Your Basenji

By Evelyn M. (Grannie) Green

Compiled and Edited by
William W. Denlinger and R. Annabel Rathman

Cover design by
Bruce Parker

DENLINGER'S
Box 76, Fairfax, Virginia 22030

To my husband and son,
Les and Murray Green

Acknowledgments

My profuse and humble thanks to those who contributed to the material used in writing *Your Basenji:* David Streeter, Basenji Club of America historian, for historical data; F. B. (Frosty) Johnson for allowing me to report on his research findings of the barkless nature of the Basenji which are incorporated in his book, *BASENJI—Dog From The Past;* Mrs. Peggie C. Peek for her cooperation in compiling data on breed and Group winners; Miss Phyliss Elliott and John Loukota for their contribution to the black and white history of the Basenji; Jon and Susan Coe for the section on lure coursing *(The Race)* and accompanying drawing; Miss Veronica Tudor-Williams for background material and photographs of the early English history, and the other prominent English breeders whose photographs so ably illustrate the Basenjis of England; Mrs. Pat Moses for her contribution to the Hawaiian history, as well as Robert Frost and Mrs. Rex Tanaka; Malcolm McDonald, Mrs. Doreen Duffin, and Mrs. Mavis-Barbara Rundle for information for the sections on Basenjis in their individual countries; Norm Wallace for his compilation of the first 106 Basenjis registered in this country and other material; and to Major Al Braun for his contribution to the chapter Basenjis in Sports. Also to Sue Cottrell for her structural and native drawings of the Basenji; Mrs. Roberta Fredrick for her exquisite native drawings; Mrs. Ruth Shannon for her loving encouragement in my endeavor to produce a worthy and authentic record of the Basenji's emergence into civilization; also to Mr. and Mrs. Shannon for permitting me to use the portrait of Ch. Fula Sirocco of the Congo on the front cover of this book; my photographer, H. M. Green, for the lovely head study of our Penny on the back cover; my long-suffering family who overlooked my short temper, skimpy meals, and sloppy housekeeping during the writing of *Your Basenji;* and our Basenjis, the real source of inspiration.

The Author, Evelyn M. Green, more familiarly known in dogdom as "Grannie Green," is shown with a favorite Basenji, Brabar's Barintha.

Foreword

When asked to read the manuscript of Grannie Green's book, *Your Basenji*, I was delighted and highly honored. Knowing Mrs. Green's excellent writing background as well as her experience with the Basenji breed, I was aware that she was well qualified to bring forth an edition which would benefit all Basenji enthusiasts now and in years to come. We pay tribute to Denlinger's Publishers for having made so wise a choice as to select Mrs. Green to further our printed knowledge of this "most misunderstood" of The American Kennel Club recognized breeds—the Basenji.

Your Basenji, with its detailed material on the breed, will enchant readers and cause them to understand why the Basenji is fast becoming so popular a breed.

Mrs. Green possesses a background of long experience in breeding dogs, beginning with Pekingese in her early teens. Most of her adult life has been involved with her interest in promoting purebred dogs, and the last ten years in breeding Basenjis and writing about the breed exclusively in national publications.

Mrs. Green is a member of the Dog Writers Association of America, the Magnolia Basenji Club, and the Basenji Club of America, and is a former member of the BCOA Official Board as well as a member of its Hemolytic Anemia Committee. She is a charter member of the Meri-Miss Kennel Club of Meridian, Mississippi, and served as its publicity chairman during the formative years. She is also a member of the Dog Owners Association, Inc. She was a 1973 award winner in the Dog Writers Association of America annual competition for her series on hemolytic anemia in a national monthly bulletin, and she served as a committee chairman for one of the division categories for the 1975 annual DWAA competition. For a number of years, Mrs. Green authored a weekly feature column on dogs for *The Meridian Star*.

I look forward with much pleasure to owning a copy of *Your Basenji*. It will assist us who choose to own Basenjis, knowing they can outsmart us unless we stay well forward in our plans. What breed other than the Basenji is able to read your mind?

Marion R. Mangrum
A.K.C. Licensed Judge

Ch. Bushveld Black Shikari, bred and owned by Mrs. Roberta Fredrick.

Ch. Reveille Re-Up, bred by Miss Damara Bolté and owned by Mrs. Elaine Hoffmann.

Contents

A basketful of puppies sired by Ch. St. Erme Fula Falcon of the Congo x St. Erme Susan Pony.   Breeder, Mrs. A. St. Erme Cardew, England.

Selecting a Basenji Puppy

You are planning to buy a puppy and the breed you've selected is the Basenji. It is hoped that you have taken the time to become acquainted with this unique breed before reaching this critical decision. No single breed is just right for everyone. This is particularly true of the little African barkless dog. To select a Basenji because he is barkless, odorless, and meticulous in his personal habits is not enough. The Basenji's personality and characteristics are vastly different from those of his fellow canines. The Basenji is a very individual dog, and to understand his nature is to love him.

James Street's magnificent novel, *Goodbye My Lady,* which was later made into a movie, attracted many people to the little dog who laughed, cried real tears, and made delightful chortling sounds. The movie created an indelible impression on this writer, although unaware at the time that such a breed actually existed. It inspired a search to identify it, and later an inspiration to defer all-breed dog writing to that of a single breed—the Basenji. Becoming more and more engrossed in an in-depth study of the Basenji and being assigned to write profiles of prominent breeders was a learning process about the many people who had become seriously involved with Basenjis as a result of having viewed the Street movie. In one instance, an enterprising theater manager brought Basenjis on stage when the movie was shown so that the captivated audience might actually view the breed. It was this human interest element which inspired a ten-year-old girl to own and finish a Basenji the following year. Now, at fourteen, she has shown two Basenjis to championship, has established a kennel, and is breeding, showing, and selling championship-quality puppies.

Before selecting a puppy it is wise to attend dog shows, observe Basenji class judging at the shows, and confer with breeders and professional handlers. It is helpful to subscribe to the Basenji breed magazine, to familiarize oneself with the prominent Basenji bloodlines, and to evaluate show results—especially those of consistent winners.

9

Eight-week-old puppy, Pero's Premadona (now a champion), bred by Mr. and Mrs. J. H. Shannon and owned by Della Biggs.

For each breed recognized by The American Kennel Club, a Standard of the breed is established. The Standard describes the characteristics required in a perfect specimen of the breed, and its provisions serve as guidelines for evaluating the conformation of the breed. It is essential to become thoroughly familiar with the Standard of the Basenji (which is included in the chapter which follows), paying special attention to designated faults, and to learn to interpret the Standard correctly.

Paramount to the purchase of a puppy, the prospective buyer must decide whether he is interested in securing a pet, a compan-

Litter brothers and sisters sired by Ch. St. Erme Fula Falcon of the Congo x Dormtiki Domewood Delicious. Breeder, Dormtiki Kennels, Mrs. C. W. White, England.

ion, a utilitarian dog, or one with show potential. Breeders of integrity can better assist the buyer if they are aware of the purpose for which the puppy is being sought. A pet or companion type puppy does not mean one with obvious faults—certainly not one with physical deformity or in poor health. The health and general physical condition of pet-type puppies should be on a par with those of litter mates of show potential.

Should the buyer be interested in purchasing a puppy to train for hunting, tracking, or coursing, he should keep in mind the stamina, the bone structure, and the alertness of the animal. It is advisable, when buying for such purposes, to contact a breeder who hunts with Basenjis and trains them. There are reputable kennels specializing in breeding and training dogs for hunting as well as in showing in conformation or competing in obedience.

When selecting a show-quality puppy, the buyer must be thorough in investigating the reliability and integrity of breeders whom he expects to contact. The first-time owner of a purebred dog is exquisitely at the mercy of the breeder when it comes to determining a puppy's potential at maturity, for there are stages of growth that make it extremely difficult for a novice to determine long-range potential. Also, one should be fully cognizant of the "going sale price" of puppies, for whatever purpose they are purchased. Beware of the "bargain" breeder!

Above all, avoid puppy mill breeders and others who are in the business of breeding and selling dogs merely for the purpose of making a profit and with no thought as to quality of the dogs produced or the welfare of the breed. Often the health of puppies from such sources is exceedingly poor from lack of routine care such as proper immunization and elimination of parasites, and from failure to provide sanitary living conditions and proper diet. Such breeders may be guilty of too close inbreeding, greatly reducing the stamina of the puppies and thus making them more subject to debilitating diseases and congenital deformities. Many of the matings are promiscuous, so the identity of the sire and dam is dubious. Registration certificates, should they be available, may be inaccurate and sometimes even falsified.

Actually, the novice with no previous experience with dogs would do better to buy an adult dog first. Later, having acquired more knowledge of the breed and its care and training, he would be better able to avoid the pitfalls that await the first-time buyer.

What is a buyer entitled to receive from the breeder when he purchases a dog? This one question has caused more problems and grief than any other concerning a purchase, assuming the buyer did receive a healthy dog with no obvious abnormalities. If a registered puppy is purchased, the buyer is entitled to receive either an individual registration certificate or a litter registration certificate issued by The American Kennel Club and properly signed by the breeder. The completed certificate, with the appropriate fee, must be mailed to the A.K.C. for transfer of ownership, either by the breeder or the new owner. After the transaction is recorded, the A.K.C. will mail the certificate to the new owner. Along with the registration certificate, it is mandatory that the breeder provide a pedigree of the puppy which the breeder attests to being true and accurate. This is the puppy's "family tree."

There have been instances where a puppy or an adult dog has been sold to a novice and an additional price has been asked for the "papers." This is highly unethical. Except in cases where the breeder is well known to the buyer and his reputation for honesty and integrity is impeccable, no money should be exchanged until the buyer has received these vital documents. Along with the registration certificate and pedigree, the breeder should provide health records and any pertinent data concerning immunization. Many breeders also include feeding, housing, and training instructions, a short history of the breed, and perhaps a copy of the breed magazine. Since a crate is essential to a Basenji, some breeders include a crate in the sale price and make a gift of the proper size training lead. These courtesies are greatly appreciated, and, most of all, give the new owner the feeling that the breeder really cares for the future welfare of the puppy. Buying a puppy is no frivolous matter; it is a transaction of grave concern for the buyer, the seller, and the puppy.

If the distance to the kennel is not too great, the buyer will find it a delightful experience to go there, make his selection, and transport the puppy to his new home by automobile. However, this is not always feasible. If the kennel is at a distance and the puppy is to be shipped, plane accommodations should be made which will schedule the arrival in the shortest possible time and preferably non-stop. If a non-stop flight is not available, then the flight should be scheduled with as few transfers or layovers as possible. The buyer should be advised of the exact day of shipment and given the flight number and schedule and the anticipated arrival time so there will be no waiting period with the puppy unattended at the airport or the freight office—which could be a traumatic experience for a young puppy. The new owner should advise the breeder promptly, preferably by telephone, of the puppy's arrival. In the event the puppy does not arrive on schedule, the breeder should be notified so that he can take immediate steps to have the airline locate the puppy and expedite his arrival.

The puppy's introduction to his new home creates a lasting and indelible impression. The reception he receives determines how well and how quickly he will adapt himself to his new surroundings. After the puppy has relieved himself, he should be provided with a cool drink of water in the place where his bowl will customarily be kept. Then, after his nerves and "tummy" have settled a bit, a small amount of food may be offered. Meanwhile, the crate will have been installed in a permanent position. This will be the puppy's "house," his security. No one, child or adult, should rush the puppy, smother him with affection, or attempt to play with him roughly. He should be given time to sniff about and become acquainted with his new home and his family. Ten to one, with the solace of drink, food, and "house," the puppy will curl up contentedly for a short nap, and then awaken refreshed and ready to become a part of his new world. From the beginning, a routine of feeding, exercise, and leisure with the family should be established and followed strictly. This is vital to the puppy's continued growth and well-being.

Should there be children in the family, especially young ones or those of any age who have not been exposed to dogs previously, they should be instructed thoroughly in their behavior toward the newcomer prior to the puppy's arrival. Many a young puppy has been turned into a snarling or cowed dog as a result of unintentional abuse from children—or adults, for that matter. Tender, loving care (TLC) is the code for a happy puppy and a delighted family.

Next comes the puppy's first visit to the veterinarian, and hopefully it will be a visit in the full meaning of the word—a let's-get-acquainted period—and preferably within forty-eight hours of the puppy's arrival at his new home. Most veterinarians, even the very busy ones, prefer to see a puppy the first time on a nonmedical basis which can also be utilized to transfer the puppy's health records so that follow-up immunizations can be scheduled. There is nothing so shocking to the nervous system of a puppy as to be taken to an animal hospital for the first time, and dumped on a cold, slippery examining table, only to be poked, prodded, and perhaps inoculated by strange hands. How much better that the puppy go "visiting" that first time to make a new friend!

Ch. Reveille Reliant, bred by Miss Damara Bolté and owned by John P. and Joan Harper.

Ch. Fula Sirocco of the Congo, bred by Miss Veronica Tudor-Williams and owned by Mr. and Mrs. J. H. Shannon.

Ch. Sirius Flare-Up To Majita with Junior Handler Chris Putscher. Co-owned by Chris and her father, W. E. Putscher.

The Adult Basenji

Purchasing an adult Basenji is a very different story from that of selecting a puppy. Again it is to be hoped that the prospective purchaser will have acquired more than a desire to own a Basenji—more than a smattering of knowledge of the breed. It is to be hoped that he will have informed himself of reputable breeders and become acquainted, at least pictorially, with current winning dogs as well as the ancestral bloodlines which produced them. This is not meant to imply that it necessarily takes champion bred to champion to produce quality dogs, but it does take bloodlines on both sides (sire and dam) that are compatible and therefore capable of producing champion quality progeny, free from hereditary and congenital impairment. Moreover, it takes an insight into the genetics of good breeding practices to mate dogs properly so that the good points are balanced rather than exaggerated and the poor qualities are minimized or corrected. All of which can be summed up in the necessity of the prospective buyer having made a comprehensive study of the breed Standard to the extent that he can use it as a slide rule to evaluate the whole dog. This is the purpose in presenting the skeletal drawing of the Basenji—to acquaint the reader with the actual bone structure of the breed. The second drawing depicts the Basenji as a representative of the breed. And last, "Mr. Wrong" illustrates many of the faults and undesirable physical qualities of a poor specimen. Faults such as these are usually hereditary factors which will reproduce themselves.

In selecting an adult Basenji, the first thing to do is to consider the physical characteristics of the dog in relation to the requirements detailed in the breed Standard. The next is to survey the generations behind the dog for their conformance to the Standard—or the reverse—and also for outstanding faults and hereditary or congenital diseases.

Over a period of years, changes may be made in the wording of a breed Standard—either for clarification or because of evolutionary changes in the breed. Consequently, it is important that the Standard used in evaluating a dog be the current one for the breed. The current Standard of the Basenji, approved by The American Kennel Club on June 8, 1954, follows:

15

STANDARD OF THE BASENJI

Characteristics—The Basenji should not bark, but is not mute. The wrinkled forehead and the swift, tireless running gait (resembling a racehorse trotting full out) are typical of the breed.

General Appearance—The Basenji is a small, lightly built, short backed dog, giving the impression of being high on the leg compared to its length. The wrinkled head must be proudly carried, and the whole demeanor should be one of poise and alertness.

Head and Skull—The skull is flat, well chiseled and of medium width, tapering towards the eyes. The foreface should taper from eye to muzzle and should be shorter than the skull. Muzzle, neither coarse nor snipy, but with rounded cushions. Wrinkles should appear upon the forehead, and be fine and profuse. Side wrinkles are desirable, but should never be exaggerated with dewlap.

Nose—Black greatly desired. A pinkish tinge should not penalize an otherwise first class specimen, but it should be discouraged in breeding.

Eyes—Dark hazel, almond shaped, obliquely set and far seeing.

Ears—Small, pointed and erect, of fine texture, set well forward on top of head.

Mouth—Teeth must be level with scissors bite.

Neck—Of good length, well crested and slightly full at base of throat. It should be well set into flat, laid back shoulders.

Forequarters—The chest should be deep and of medium width. The legs straight with clean, fine bone, long forearm and well defined sinews. Pasterns should be of good length, straight and flexible.

Body—The body should be short and the back level. The ribs well sprung, with plenty of heart room, deep brisket, short coupled, and ending in a definite waist.

Hindquarters—Should be strong and muscular, with hocks well let down, turned neither in nor out, with long second thighs.

Feet—Small, narrow and compact, with well arched toes.

Tail—Should be set on top and curled tightly over to either side.

Coat—Short and silky. Skin very pliant.

Color—Chestnut red (the deeper the better) or pure black, or black and tan, all with white feet, chest and tail tip. White legs, white blaze and white collar optional.

Weight—Bitches 22 pounds approximately. Dogs 24 pounds approximately.

Size—Bitches 16 inches and dogs 17 inches from the ground to the top of the shoulder. Bitches 16 inches and dogs 17 inches from the front of the chest to the farthest point of the hindquarters.

Faults—Coarse skull or muzzle. Domed or peaked skull. Dewlap. Round eyes. Low set ears. Overshot or undershot mouths. Wide chest. Wide behind. Heavy bone. Creams, shaded or off colors, other than those defined above, should be heavily penalized.

Unfortunately, Standards are not interpreted in the same way by all individuals. This fact has presented handicaps to both breeders and judges. For instance, the Standard describes the mouth as "Teeth level with scissors bite." Since it is an impossibility for teeth to be both "level" and "with scissors bite," the Standard needs clarification. It is this writer's opinion that the scissors bite is correct for the Basenji.

16

Some concern has been expressed that today's Basenji has deviated from the Standard to become a larger and a heavier boned dog than described in the Standard. Some of the current winning dogs exceed the designated height by as much as three to four inches. Basenjis of this build would never survive the jungle life of their forebears, which required a small, agile dog, tough enough to withstand the rugged life but light enough to leap up and down over the tall grasses in search of game. Recently, there has been an obvious effort among a few breeders to reduce the size and bone structure of non-conformists, with the result that they have produced Basenjis too light in bone and with a daintiness of build usually ascribed to Toy breeds. Their African "cousins" would never look upon these dogs as their kin. But there are other breeders, bless them, who cling tenaciously to the Standard and they shall be the Basenjis' salvation.

Both eye color and eye shape have come in for criticism, now and again, as deviating from the description in the Standard. Occasionally a yellowish or light tan eye color will slip into a breeding program, as well as round eyes, which detract from the whole character of the facial expression and most certainly eliminate the far seeing effect which typifies the questing nature of the Basenji. Such dogs should definitely not be shown and most certainly should be eliminated from breeding programs.

Deviations from the proper ear set and the correct size of the ear have presented problems, too. The small, erect ear, set well forward on the top of the head, emphasizes the poise and alertness which are so typical of the breed. A broad or domed skull with accompanying large ears tending to flare out, giving a fly-away appearance, results in a heavy look to the head, which should be elegant in appearance.

The personality and temperament of the Basenji are as unique as his barkless nature—though let me hasten to clarify, the Basenji is far from mute. He perhaps has a wider variety of vocal sounds than any of the other breeds, but he is judicious in using them. The Basenji yodels when he is happy. His mating call rings out loud and clear when bitches come in season. He growls when he or his human family are threatened. He is a loyal, loving little dog, a delightful companion, eager and willing to please. But he is his own master and he will not respond to a harsh voice or abusive hands.

The Basenji coat has been cause for considerable concern in some instances, especially in the tri-colors and the black and

Skeletal drawing of the Basenji by Sue Cottrell.

The Basenji, according to the Standard. Drawing by Sue Cottrell.

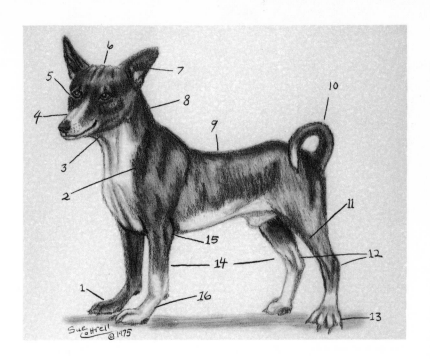

Mr. Wrong—faults according to the Standard: 1—flat, thin feet, mismatched; 2—loaded, straight shoulders; 3—dewlap; 4—long, snipy muzzle; 5—round, light eyes; 6—wide, domed skull, lack of wrinkle; 7—large ears, poor ear set; 8—short, heavy neck; 9—"dippy" back, long top line; 10—loose tail curl, poor tail set; 11—straight stifles; 12—cowhocks; 13—splayed feet; 14—short legs; 15—out at elbows; 16—down in pasterns. Drawing by Sue Cottrell.

Ch. Ashanti's Even Beauty, owned by Pat and John Loukota.

whites. In both cases, the body coat should be fine and silky with a patent leather sheen, and a deep pure black in color. No tan markings should be evidenced on the body, especially on the shoulders and flanks.

As in all breeds, there are hereditary diseases which may afflict the Basenji. The three most prevalent are hemolytic anemia, persistent pupillary membrane, and diabetes.

Hemolytic anemia, more commonly referred to as HA, is a hereditary disease of the blood. A genetic deformity of the enzymes, HA is fatal if the disease actually exists in the dog. However, a dog may be a carrier of HA but show no physical effects of

Ch. Shikari's Black Mamba, owned by Mrs. Pat Church, Shikari Kennels.

the disease. Unfortunately, a carrier may propagate HA through its progeny. Hemolytic anemia can be eliminated provided all breeders have their breeding stock tested at approved testing centers and avoid using afflicted dogs and carriers in their breeding programs. When buying a Basenji, either a puppy or an adult, the buyer should ask the breeder to furnish him with the test results from a Basenji Club of America Testing Center. It is desirable to have two generations tested clear of carrying HA. This is to eliminate any margin of error in testing. It is essential that only clear dogs be used for breeding. The cost of testing, along with the possibility of the most promising puppies being carriers, makes the using of carriers both expensive and discouraging.

Persistent pupillary membrane (PPM) is a condition of the eye in which the pupillary membrane (a substance covering the pupils of a puppy's eyes before birth) has failed to absorb before the puppy is whelped. Absorption may be only partially complete, and shreds of the membrane will then be found, upon clinical examination, to extend across the pupillary opening (pupil of the eye), and may be attached to an opaque spot on the lens. It is not uncommon, in fact, to find these membranous strands in the eyes of young puppies. In some cases they will disappear.

Testing for PPM by the slit beam method is performed by an ophthalmologist when the puppy is six months old or older. This is the preferred method of testing and provides an absolutely reliable diagnosis.

Diabetes, the "sneaky" disease, exists in both man and animal, although it is not so prevalent in the latter. When diagnosed in its early stages, diabetes can be treated in man; it is more difficult to control in animals. There are two types of diabetes. The one we are concerned about in Basenjis is more commonly known as "sugar diabetes." This is an elevation of the sugar content in the blood resulting from an inadequacy of the enzyme insulin, which is furnished by the pancreas. As a result, the kidneys cannot handle the sugar overflow.

Symptoms of diabetes include increased appetite, persistent loss of weight, enlargement of the abdominal area, marked thirst, abnormal consumption of water, and frequency of urination, which is sometimes uncontrollable. Should any of these symptoms persist, a blood sugar test (the same as that used in humans) is indicated. Should diabetes be found in any animal, it should be eliminated from the breeding program because of the tendency of the disease to recur in succeeding generations.

Trypheana of the Congo.

Ch. Lepper's Red Pepper.

Scene from movie based on book by James Street, *Goodbye My Lady*, starring Brandon d'Wilde.

Personality of the Basenji

When the Basenji was first introduced to civilization, he was said to have a problem in adjusting to the requisites of his new world and its life style. Such, however, was not the case in his prompt acceptance of his home surroundings. Accustomed as the Basenji was to being a companion to man, his instincts were to adapt himself to the habits of his master. It is understandable, however, that the little bush dog, as the Basenji was commonly called, should have been confused at the onset with the rapid flow of events that moved him from primitive surroundings to the sophistication of civilization.

Perhaps it was his introduction to training for the show ring and to contacts with breeds hitherto unknown to him, that gained the Basenji a reputation of being a "problem dog," sometimes physically defensive. To those who know and understand the breed, he is a lovable ham, eager to please, willing to learn, quick to comprehend, and exceedingly loyal. In his natural setting, the African dog was accustomed to receiving commands only from his master. Then upon his emergence into another world, he was exposed to many people who expected the same attitude of him that he had formerly reserved solely for his master. He received instructions from total strangers—class judges, competing exhibitors, and professional handlers. It is no small wonder that he was wont to rebel at times. He was confused! Meanwhile, the damage was done. Judges proclaimed their "fear" of the elegant little Hound and were loathe to lay hands upon him for examination for fear of retaliation. Today, that early problem has been resolved. The Basenji has indeed adapted quickly. He has excelled in obedience competition, accumulated notable wins in conformation shows, and is rapidly proving himself in the hunting field—his natural habitat.

Several qualities of the Basenji have caused him to be likened to the Siamese cat. Like the feline, the Basenji is vastly independent and is intolerant of coddling but very affectionate on his own initiative, though never to the extent that it will ruffle his natural dignity. Personal cleanliness is instinctive with the Basenji, as it is with a cat. Coming indoors from an outing, he might be stained or muddied. His first concern is to clean himself thoroughly, licking painstakingly and roughly at the grime. Give him thirty minutes to complete his toilet and he will emerge sparkling clean. That is the nature of the Basenji. His cleanliness also contributes to his lack of odor, making him doubly acceptable as a family member.

I've heard of only one incident where a Basenji was unable to rid himself of a repugnant odor without human assistance. Humorous as it is now, it created a very odoriferous problem at the time. A young couple was in the habit of including their Basenji, Wiggins, on pleasure outings. This occasion was a bicycle trip in the Texas countryside. Riding alternately in the basket with Walt or Nancy, Wiggins would make wayside excursions to investigate the rural life.

As the couple and the bouyant Wiggins neared the college campus, homeward bound, the mischievous dog attempted a premature acquaintance with a skunk, which rewarded his friendly overtures by spraying him thoroughly. Disgustedly, Wiggins tried ridding himself of the offensive odor, but his frantic efforts were of no avail. Walt and Nancy decided it would be quicker to carry him the short distance home in one of the bicycle baskets. They flipped a coin to determine who would be the conveyor of the much chastened and embarrassed rambler. Nancy lost! It took repeated bathing with scented shampoos, augmented by the lavishing of fragrant cologne, to diminish the odor even slightly. A frantic call to Nancy's mother, a thousand miles away, gave them the simple solution—a dousing with tomato juice. Wiggins has since kept a respectable distance from meandering skunks.

The prankish nature of the Basenji, along with evidence of his hunting instincts, was forever immortalized one chilly autumn evening when our son returned from hunting. He laid his quarry on the edge of the kitchen counter while he rid himself of outer clothing and muddied boots. Returning to dress the squirrels, he found one missing. Both house dogs were seated innocently on the sofa, ears pricked alertly as they watched with absorbed interest our frantic search. The missing squirrel was discovered eventually, stashed neatly in the rear of a dog crate and obviously intended for a midnight snack.

Although the Basenji has many vocal expressions, he is quiet on the whole but uses his voice as a means of expressing varying emotions. His growl is deep and meaningful; be it directed at man or beast, the offender had best beware. His rebuttal to threat or attack is swift and ruthless, and he is especially protective of his human family. It is this quality which makes him an excellent guard or watch dog. It was our first Basenji who gave us an example. Mitzi, forsaking the crate provided for her, had chosen to sleep with us. We were awakened abruptly one night in the "wee small hours" by an ominous, low-key growl. Mitzi's hind feet were braced on the side rail of our bed, her forefeet planted on the sill of the open window. She was peering intently outdoors, her body aquiver with rage. Occasionally she would scratch the screen furiously. We galvanized into action in time to see a crouched figure fleeing past the window. Later we were to learn there had been a series of burglaries in the neighborhood and ours was the only home escaping vandalism—due to the vigilance of a Basenji.

Swift as is the Basenji on the defensive, he also has a social nature. He delights in friends coming to call and will invite himself to sleep with overnight guests. He is the genial host, considering it his duty to attend to the creature comforts of "his guests." The keynote, we have learned, is the tone of the human voice used in greeting. If the voice is welcoming, the visitor is received graciously by our Basenji. When he is uncertain of their welcome, he is on alert until he is sure of our reception of the callers.

Never underestimate the intelligence of our African dog. He's a quick thinker, often outwitting less agile human minds. He'll not hold a grudge should he consider himself neglected but will plan his reprisal cunningly and execute it when least expected. It will usually be in the form of a misdemeanor such as chewing a favorite shoe or, with utter disdain, wetting the bed. Inevitably his revenge is discovered when he is again on his best behavior, probably pressing his affectionate attentions on the object of his punishment.

The same quick thinking enables the Basenji to excel in obedience training, but it is always wise for the owner to allow the dog to observe a few sessions prior to enrollment. A Basenji likes to know what is expected of him and is mortified by being placed in a situation where he appears in a bad light. He will retaliate by taking "French leave" or become inexpressibly stubborn. It takes a keen mind to keep abreast of a Basenji's reasoning and, hopefully, to remain two jumps ahead of his activity.

Ch. Il-Se-Ott Golden
Majorette, U.D.T.

Major Al Braun and two companions view the results of a day's hunting with a pair
of alert Basenjis.

Wandra Belinda, forward,
with Ch. Congoglen
Kirsty.

The Basenji in Sports

By heredity and environment, the Basenji is a hunting dog. Historians reveal that in his native land, he hunted with his master to provide meat for the table. Some have implied that the Basenji himself would be served as the "main course" when game, fish, or fowl was not forthcoming. Yet, with all his early attributes for hunting prowess, the Basenji is just now coming into his own in this country. His full potential is yet to be recognized and utilized. This fleet footed, swift running Hound is the most versatile of the hunting dogs, in that he hunts both by sight and by scent and can readily switch from one method to the other in a single outing. Admittedly, his manner of pointing is a bit different from that of his competitors—but it is equally effective.

Al Braun, along with wife Kitty, of Henty P'Kenya Kennels, Reg., is the acknowledged authority in this country on training Basenjis for hunting. Major Braun first hunted with Basenjis in Madrid, Spain, when he was stationed there with the Air Force. At that time he owned a Basenji that he had obtained while stationed in England. The dog had spent his puppyhood in a London suburb, reaching maturity in the Brauns' Madrid penthouse apartment. A seasoned hunter, Al was invited on an expedition with some newly made Spanish friends who hunted with Ibizan Hounds. You can imagine with what little enthusiasm he was greeted when he arrived with his untrained Basenji, Circus Boy.

The object of the hunt was the perdiz, a game bird native of Spain and an exceedingly tricky quarry. It was a cold, wet, windy day when Circus Boy was released with the Ibizans. When the dogs settled down to hunting and flushing birds, Circus Boy began to imitate them. After several hours of strenuous work, the Ibizans were exhausted. Not so with Circus Boy. He was still fresh and eager, so the men continued hunting with him alone and acquired several more birds. By then it was time for the tired hunters to call it a day. Circus Boy was carried, literally protesting, to the car, far from spent.

Basenjis are trained for hunting much as any other breed, asserts Major Braun. First comes obedience training, and then the dog is introduced to hunting and is trained by voice command. A Basenji

Joyfred Forest King, owned by Fred Jones, England is seen leaping the net on a hunting expedition with Mr. Jones.

will hunt any game or fowl—providing he has first been trained to obey his master. His native instinct provides the additional necessary ability.

Major Braun stresses that to train a Basenji takes a thorough understanding of the breed's nature in order to teach the dog to obey happily. "It is almost impossible," he states firmly, "for a Basenji to do your bidding through force alone. He will eventually obey but resentfully and with reluctance. The preferred results can be obtained through patient, loving firmness. He must be taught that you are the boss and the one he must obey but also that you do love and understand him."

It is Major Braun's theory that it is best to select a puppy from a litter that comes of parents which have demonstrated hunting desires and abilities. In such a litter, there will be puppies which have displayed hunting instincts since infancy—such as watching birds perched or flying, perhaps freezing in their tracks when birds are sighted, or even going into the very unique Basenji point with forelegs flat to the ground and rear high in a crouch. Or they may streak toward the prey and flush it.

When training a puppy for hunting, the initial objective is establishment of a relationship comparable to that of parent-teacher, and then making informal play a part of his discipline. Never work a dog when he is hungry nor when he has just been fed. Work hard with him with regular frequency, and you will have a young dog which will hunt and flush game eagerly. A cap gun is best used in

Joyfred Forest King emerges triumphant with his quarry.

early training to accustom the dog to the sound of a gun. A fly rod with a wing attached to an eight-foot-long line is an excellent training tool to use in familiarizing the dog to the scent, feel, and sight of birds. Thus the groundwork is laid. The rest is working the dog—more experience in actual hunting with the dog.

Basenjis have long excelled in obedience despite the fact that many trainers have underestimated the high I.Q. of the breed, attributing the Basenji's restlessness and lack of attention to his inability to comprehend basic training. In actuality, the dog becomes bored with the slow pace of initial training. Many Basenjis have advanced in degrees from Companion Dog (C.D.) to Companion Dog Excellent (C.D.X.), and a first for a Basenji was attained in 1974 when Rex Tanaka's Ch. Il-Se-Ott Majorette (Tammy) became the first Basenji in the world to earn all obedience degrees offered by The American Kennel Club along with the championship title in conformation. It took six and one-half years of consistent training to achieve this, but consistent training paid off.

It would bear repeating that the first Basenji in this country to receive the C.D. degree was the Alexander Phemister's Barrie. Among the breeders who have contributed to the Basenji's accomplishments in obedience training, in addition to Major Braun, are Robert and Cecelia Wozniak, Jo Ann Weller, Dorothy Brashier, Lois Cox, George and Jane Larsen, William and Doris Kukuk, Rex Tanaka, and many others.

When the Minnesota Basenji Club held its third Basenji field trial match, a puppy field trial fun match was included. Five pheasants were planted in well-concealed areas in order for the dogs to experience their first actual hunting. They performed creditably, their points varying from a flush point and steady stalking to the classic Basenji point.

Basenjis are making a place for themselves in lure coursing, too. Results of two meets held by the Puget Sound Saluki Club in Marymoor Park, Washington, on June 22 and August 24, 1974, show Basenjis placed eighth in rank with 54.0 seconds running time in the June race, advancing to sixth place with 38.4 seconds running time in the August race. This, according to John Charles Coe in the Basenji Club of America *Bulletin,* is an indication of the lure coursing abilities of the Basenji.

The following is a mythical story by Mr. Coe which exemplifies the thrill of lure coursing, which is fast becoming popular with Basenji sports enthusiasts. The accompanying drawing was executed by his wife, Susan Coe.

The Race

The August evening is charged with excitement as the hounds are led to the starting line. Now it's the Basenjis' turn and they're ready. Sinewy muscles tense along the hard lines of these well-conditioned hunters. Their hunter's eyes, falcon-like, are fixed on a point then yards ahead where their prey lies.

The prey, only a tatter of rabbit pelt, remains unalive and unimpressed. It has not yet been given life and legs by the magic of the lure machine. This salvaged car starter motor and reel have not yet felt the lure operator's command to bring life and movement to the lure through the 660 yards of taut towline that circles the course around four horizontally placed pulleys. The pulleys are spiked to the ground at three corners of the double soccer field with one intermediately located to round out the far turn. This arrangement brings the racers completely around the field. They end up at their approximate starting point, into the arms of their waiting owners.

The starter signals readiness to the lure machine operator and the crowd quiets. Those who have seen Basenjis run before are telling friends, "Watch the bitch in red." "Watch those little dogs"; comes a reply, "Can they run?"

We've unhooked the Basenjis' leads now and strain to hold them by their leather collars at the starting line. The starter's hand is up. "Tally ho," comes the cry and the dogs are off, leaving flying shreds of turf behind them.

It's a good start. Akua cuts inside immediately behind Tembo, her kennel mate, red colors flashing in the late light as she swerves. Already the Basenjis' pounding feet are inaudible; they're closing fast on the first turn. From this distance the lure appears barely ahead of the hounds and scarcely moving. Suddenly it flashes away at right angles as it rounds the first pulley. The Basenjis, who have been racing all summer, are not caught off guard. In fact, little Akua, now in her third year of racing, takes the turn at full speed. Her body is almost horizontal as she banks into the curve and slips ahead of her heavier companion. Tembo, easily distinguished by his larger size and longer stride, falls obediently in line behind Akua. Suni, Akua's lovely daughter, is a close third.

The hounds are stretching out into their natural single file coursing formation taught them by generations of hunters, far beyond memory or number. This allows the leader to pick the easiest path for all and ensures, even though the quarry cut without warning to the side, only the front runner would be out of position. They would run abreast only when the prey was almost within reach.

The second turn is just ahead, again the hounds are ready, turning as the lure flashes away in a 60° right turn. Knowing the course as they do, the Basenjis could easily cut well inside the corners and head off the lure, disqualifying themselves and running a serious danger of becoming entangled in the speeding towline ahead of the rabbit, yet they continue to run true. Perhaps something deep inside them tells them this is real or perhaps they run for the pure joy of the chase, celebrating in their own speed, grace, and endurance.

The dogs have now run about one-half of the 660 yard course. They are coasting a bit down the back stretch, conserving energy yet moving with surprising speed, even viewed at this distance. Their racing vests, red, blue, and yellow, haven't changed order since the first turn and the spectators are anticipating a highly predictable outcome.

Akua is now twenty yards ahead of her "lord and master" while he leads Suni by an equal distance. Akua hasn't Tembo's power nor his good shoulders and superbly angulated rear quarters, but she has excellent balance and is in terrific condition. Equally important, she is the proud hunter, the immaculate master of the chase. She will *not* be beaten!

The lure is approaching the next to last pulley and again the Basenjis are showing their professional mastery of footwork and timing, preparing for the curve. Suddenly, in an instant, the lure stops! It has hung up on the pulley and the operator hurriedly stops the two motors! Instantly the dogs shoot past, over-running the snagged lure and braking furiously as they attempt to reverse themselves. With startling speed they are back after the fouled lure.

Suni is first back, having been last in line, and makes a determined dive for the prey. To her amazement, it leaps wildly from her grasp. She's pulled it free! The accumulated tension in the nylon monofilament towline draws the rabbit skin in a great leap over the heads of the two onrushing Basenjis. Akua, with instant reflexes, leaps recklessly at the passing lure, twisting and reversing herself in mid-air even as she leaps. She has it!

The impact flips her like a hooked salmon, yet she holds on. The strain is too great for the thin rabbit pelt and a great piece comes away in her mouth as the lure again breaks free.

Tembo has recovered almost as agilely as his doughty little kennel mate, but the lure is already beyond his reach. Once more the race is on!

Akua picks herself up, shaking her head and fighting for breath as Suni shoots past. "Come on, Ma, don't let it get away!" Tembo is now twenty yards ahead of the two bitches, but in his excitement he's forgotten the last turn. Almost too late he sees the lure cut away at 90° toward the finish line only 100 yards away. Furiously he brakes, sending knots of sod flying from under his tearing feet. His powerful rear quarters drive in front of the turn at full speed, but he knows Akua has gained on him. Down the line they drive, with seemingly impossible reserves.

Akua pulls even with Tembo. A glace at her grinning face and bright eyes tells him again that she will win, but lure and finish line are just ahead—if only he can hold out! He renews his drive, pulling slightly ahead, but Akua will not be beaten! The lure hits the finish line and the operator kills the motor. The Basenjis are on it again and Akua has it! Immediately Tembo has the other end with Suni close behind. Proudly they jointly parade their prize before the crowd, then stop for a three-way tug of war. The only way to separate these keen little hounds from the lure is by waving another rabbit skin before them!

Finally we have them back on leads, headed back to the car. Another race is over. If the light holds, they may get two more chances tonight!

A trio of racing Basenjis owned by the Keith Jordans of Congoglen Kennels, New South Wales. Left to right are Wandra Belinda, Ch. Congobell Nutmeg, and Ch. Wandra Ducat.

Left to right, Ch. Pyramid's Enchantress, C.D., with Ch. Pyramid's Kayzu, C.D., owned by Harry and Violette Lazarenko, Canada.

The Race—Akua leaps recklessly at the passing lure. Drawing by Susan Coe.

Grooming and
General Coat Care

Although coat types, textures, and patterns may seem purely arbitrary matters of little consequence, they are among the important characteristics that distinguish one breed from another. Actually, each breed has been developed to serve a specific purpose, and the coat that is considered typical for the breed is also the one most appropriate for the dog's specialized use—be it as guard, hunting companion, herder, or pet. A knowledge of the breed Standard approved by The American Kennel Club is helpful to the owner who takes pride in owning a well-groomed dog, typical of its breed.

Dogs with short, smooth coats (such as the Weimaraner, Basset, Beagle, smooth Dachshund and Chihuahua) usually shed only moderately and their coats require little routine grooming other than thorough brushing with a bristle brush or hound glove. For exhibition in the show ring, the whiskers, or "feelers," are trimmed close to the muzzle, but no other trimming is needed.

The wire coat of the Airedale, Wire Fox Terrier, Miniature Schnauzer, or Wirehaired Dachshund should be stripped or plucked in show trim at regular intervals. The dog can then be kept well groomed by thorough combing and brushing.

Curly coated breeds such as the Curly Coated Retriever, and the American and Irish Water Spaniels, generally require no special coat care other than frequent brushing. True curly coated breeds are very curly indeed and are not to be confused with breeds such as the Golden Retriever, Gordon Setter, Brittany Spaniel, and English Springer Spaniel, which have slightly curled or wavy coats of somewhat silky texture. The longer hair, or "feathers," typically found on tail, legs, ears, and chest of these breeds should be trimmed slightly to make the outline neater.

(UPPER LEFT) Wire brush (RIGHT) Bristle brush
(LOWER LEFT) Comb—Hound glove.

They are not "trimmed to pattern," however, as are such long-haired breeds as the Kerry Blue Terrier and the Poodle, which, when shown in the breed ring, must be clipped and trimmed in the patterns specified in the breed Standards.

The Longhaired Dachshund, the Borzoi, and the Yorkshire Terrier have long but comparatively silky coats, whereas the Newfoundland and the Rough Collie have long straight coats with rather harsh texture. Long coats must be kept brushed out thoroughly to eliminate mats and snarls.

The dog should be taught from puppyhood that a grooming session is a time for business, not for play. He should be handled gently, though, for it is essential to avoid hurting him in any way. Grooming time should be pleasant for both dog and master.

Tools required vary with the breed, but always include combs, brushes, and nail clippers and files. Combs should have wide-spaced teeth with rounded ends so that the dog's skin will not be scratched accidentally. For the same reason, brushes with natural bristles are usually preferable to those with synthetic bristles that may be too fine and sharp.

A light, airy, pleasant place in which to work is desirable, and it is of the utmost importance that neither dog nor master be distracted by other dogs, cats, or people. Consequently, it is usually preferable that grooming be done indoors.

Particularly for large or medium breeds, a sturdy grooming table is desirable. Many owners hold small puppies or Toy dogs during grooming sessions, athough it is better if they, too, are groomed on a table. Large and medium size dogs should be taught to jump onto the table and to jump off again when grooming is completed. Small dogs must be lifted on and off to avoid falls and possible injury. The dog should stand while the back and upper portions of the body are groomed, and lie on his side while underparts of his body are brushed, nails clipped, etc.

Before each session, the dog should be permitted to relieve himself. Once grooming is begun, it is important to avoid keeping the dog standing so long that he becomes tired. If a good deal of grooming is needed, it should be done in two or more short periods.

It is almost impossible to brush too much, and show dogs are often brushed for a full half hour a day, year round. If you cannot brush your dog every day, you should brush him a minimum of two or three times a week. Brushing removes loose skin particles and stimulates circulation, thereby improving condition of the skin. It also stimulates secretion of the natural skin oils that make the coat look healthy and beautiful.

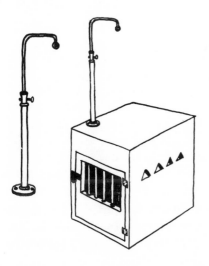

Dog crate with grooming—table top is ideal—providing rigid, well supported surface on which to groom dog, and serving as indoor kennel for puppy or grown dog. Rubber matting provides non-slip surface. Dog's collar may be attached to adjustable arm. Lightweight and readily transported yet sturdy, the crate is especially useful to owner who takes dog with him when he travels.

Before brushing, any burs adhering to the coat, as well as matted hair, should be carefully removed, using the fingers and coarse toothed comb with a gentle, teasing motion to avoid tearing the coat. The coat should first be brushed lightly in the direction in which the hair grows. Next, it should be brushed vigorously in the opposite direction, a small portion at a time, making sure the bristles penetrate the hair to the skin, until the entire coat has been brushed thoroughly and all loose soil removed. Then the coat should be brushed in the direction the hair grows, until every hair is sleekly in place.

The dog that is kept well brushed needs bathing only rarely. Once or twice a year is usually enough. Except for unusual circumstances when his coat becomes excessively soiled, no puppy under six months of age should be bathed in water. If it is necessary to bathe a puppy, extreme care must be exercised so that he will not become chilled. No dog should be bathed during cold weather and then permitted to go outside immediately. Whatever the weather, the dog should always be given a good run outdoors and permitted to relieve himself before he is bathed.

Various types of "dry baths" are available at pet supply stores. In general, they are quite satisfactory when circumstances are such that a bath in water is impractical. Dry shampoos are usually rubbed into the dog's coat thoroughly, then removed by vigorous towelling or brushing.

Before starting a water bath, the necessary equipment should be assembled. This includes a tub of appropriate size, and another tub or pail for rinse water. (A small hose with a spray nozzle—one that may be attached to the water faucet—is ideal for rinsing the dog.) A metal or plastic cup for dipping water, special dog shampoo, a small bottle of mineral or olive oil, and a supply of absorbent cotton should be placed nearby, as well as a supply of heavy towels, a wash cloth, and the dog's combs and brushes.

The amount of water required will vary according to the size of the dog, but should reach no higher than the dog's elbows. Bath water and rinse water should be slightly warmer than lukewarm, but should not be hot.

To avoid accidentally getting water in the dog's ears, place a small amount of absorbent cotton in each. With the dog standing in the tub, wet his body by using the cup to pour water over him. Take care to avoid wetting the head, and be careful to avoid getting water or shampoo in the eyes. (If you should accidentally do so, placing a few drops of mineral or olive oil in the inner corner of the eye will bring relief.) When the dog is thoroughly wet, put a small amount of shampoo on his back and work up a lather, rubbing briskly. Wash his entire body and then rinse as much of the shampoo as possible from the coat by dipping water from the tub and pouring it over the dog.

Dip the wash cloth into clean water, wring it out enough so it won't drip, then wash the dog's head, taking care to avoid the eyes. Remove the cotton from the dog's ears and sponge them gently, inside and out. Shampoo should never be used inside the ears, so if they are extremely soiled, sponge them clean with cotton saturated with mineral or olive oil. (Between baths, the ears should be cleaned frequently in the same way.)

Replace the cotton in the ears, then use the cup and container of rinse water (or hose and spray nozzle) to rinse the dog thoroughly. Quickly wrap a towel around him, remove him from the tub, and towel him as dry as possible. To avoid getting an impromptu bath yourself, you must act quickly, for once he is out of the tub, the dog will instinctively shake himself.

While the hair is still slightly damp, use a clean comb or brush to remove any tangles. If the hair is allowed to dry first, it may be completely impossible to remove them.

So far as routine grooming is concerned, the dog's eyes require little attention. Some dogs have a slight accumulation of mucus in the corner of the eyes upon waking mornings. A salt solution (1 teaspoon of table salt to one pint of warm, sterile water) can be sponged around the eyes to remove the stain. During grooming sessions it is well to inspect the eyes, since many breeds are prone to eye injury. Eye problems of a minor nature may be treated at home (see page 50), but it is imperative that any serious eye abnormality be called to the attention of the veterinarian immediately.

Feeding hard dog biscuits and hard bones helps to keep tooth surfaces clean. Slight discoloration may be readily removed by rubbing with a damp cloth dipped in salt or baking soda. The dog's head should be held firmly, the lips pulled apart gently, and the teeth rubbed lightly with the dampened cloth. Regular

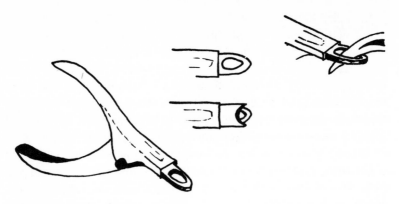

Nail trimmer—center detail shows blade cutting action. Right shows manner of inserting nail in cutter.

care usually keeps the teeth in good condition, but if tartar accumulates, it should be removed by a veterinarian.

If the dog doesn't keep his nails worn down through regular exercise on hard surfaces, they must be trimmed at intervals, for nails that are too long may cause the foot to spread and thus spoil the dog's gait. Neglected nails may even grow so long that they will grow into a circle and puncture the dog's skin. Nails can be cut easily with a nail trimmer that slides over the nail end. The cut is made just outside the faintly pink bloodline that can be seen on white nails. In pigmented nails, the bloodline is not easily seen, so the cut should be made just outside the hooklike projection on the underside of the nails. A few downward strokes with a nail file will smooth the cut surface, and, once shortened, nails can be kept short by filing at regular intervals.

Care must be taken that nails are not cut too short, since blood vessels may be accidentally severed. Should you accidentally cut a nail so short that it bleeds, apply a mild antiseptic and keep the dog quiet until bleeding stops. Usually, only a few drops of blood will be lost. But once a dog's nails have been cut painfully short, he will usually object when his feet are handled.

Nutrition

The main food elements required by dogs are proteins, fats, and carbohydrates. Vitamins A, B complex, D, and E are essential, as are ample amounts of calcium and iron. Nine other minerals are required in small amounts but are amply provided in almost any diet, so there is no need to be concerned about them.

The most important nutrient is protein and it must be provided every day of the dog's life, for it is essential for normal daily growth and replacement of body tissues burned up in daily activity. Preferred animal protein products are beef, mutton, horse meat, and boned fish. Visceral organs—heart, liver, and tripe—are good but if used in too large quantities may cause diarrhea (bones in large amounts have the same effect). Pork, particularly fat pork, is undesirable. The "meat meal" used in some commercial foods is made from scrap meat processed at high temperatures and then dried. It is not quite so nutritious as fresh meat, but in combination with other protein products, it is an acceptable ingredient in the dog's diet.

Cooked eggs and raw egg yolk are good sources of protein, but raw egg white should never be fed since it cannot be digested by the dog and may cause diarrhea. Cottage cheese and milk (fresh, dried, and canned) are high in protein, also. Puppies thrive on milk and it can well be included in the diet of older dogs, too, if mixed with meat, vegetables, and meal. Soy-bean meal, wheat germ meal, and dried brewers yeast are vegetable products high in protein and may be used to advantage in the diet.

Vegetable and animal fats in moderate amounts should be used, especially if a main ingredient of the diet is dry or kibbled food. Fats should not be used excessively or the dog may become overweight. Generally, fats should be increased slightly in the winter and reduced somewhat during warm weather.

Carbohydrates are required for proper assimilation of fats. Dog biscuits, kibble, dog meal, and other dehydrated foods are good sources of carbohydrates, as are cereal products derived from rice, corn, wheat, and ground or rolled oats.

Vegetables supply additional proteins, vitamins, and minerals, and by providing bulk are of value in overcoming constipation. Raw or cooked carrots, celery, lettuce, beets, asparagus, tomatoes, and cooked spinach may be used. They should always be chopped or ground well and mixed with the other food. Various combinations may be used, but a good home-mixed ration for the mature dog consists of two parts of meat and one each of vegetables and dog meal (or cereal product).

Dicalcium phosphate and cod-liver oil are added to puppy diets to ensure inclusion of adequate amounts of calcium and Vitamins A and D. Indiscriminate use of dietary supplements is not only unjustified but may actually be harmful and many breeders feel that their over-use in diets of extremely small breeds may lead to excessive growth as well as to overweight at maturity.

Foods manufactured by well-known and reputable food processors are nutritionally sound and are offered in sufficient variety of flavors, textures, and consistencies that most dogs will find them tempting and satisfying. Canned foods are usually "ready to eat," while dehydrated foods in the form of kibble, meal, or biscuits may require the addition of water or milk. Dried foods containing fat sometimes become rancid, so to avoid an unpalatable change in flavor, the manufacturer may not include fat in dried food but recommend its addition at the time the water or milk is added.

Candy and other sweets are taboo, for the dog has no nutritional need for them and if he is permitted to eat them, he will usually eat less of foods he requires. Also taboo are fried foods, highly seasoned foods and extremely starchy foods, for the dog's digestive tract is not equipped to handle them.

Frozen foods should be thawed completely and warmed at least to lukewarm, while hot foods should be cooled to lukewarm. Food should be in a fairly firm state, for sloppy food is difficult for the dog to digest.

Whether meat is raw or cooked makes little difference, so long as the dog is also given the juice that seeps from the meat during cooking. Bones provide little nourishment, although gnawing bones helps make the teeth strong and helps to keep tartar from accumulating on them. Beef bones, especially large knuckle bones, are best. Fish, poultry, and chop bones should never be given to dogs since they have a tendency to splinter and may puncture the dog's digestive tract.

Clean, fresh, cool water is essential to all dogs and an adequate supply should be readily available twenty-four hours a day from the time the puppy is big enough to walk. Especially during hot weather, the drinking pan should be emptied and refilled at frequent intervals.

Puppies usually are weaned by the time they are six weeks old, so when you acquire a new puppy ten to twelve weeks old, he will already have been started on a feeding schedule. The breeder should supply exact details as to number of meals per day, types and amounts of food offered, etc. It is essential to adhere to this established routine, for drastic changes in diet may produce intestinal upsets.

Until a puppy is six months old, milk formula is an integral part of the diet. A day's supply should be made up at one time and stored in the refrigerator, and the quantity needed for each meal warmed at feeding time. The following combination is good for all breeds:

1 pint whole fresh milk	1 tablespoon lime water
1 raw egg yolk, slightly beaten	1 tablespoon lactose

The two latter items (as well as cod-liver oil and dicalcium phosphate to be added to solid food) are readily available at pet supply stores and drug stores.

At twelve weeks of age the amount of formula given at each feeding will vary from three to four tablespoonfuls for the Toy breeds, to perhaps two cupfuls for the large breeds. If the puppy is on the five-meal-a-day schedule when he leaves the kennel, three of the meals (first, third, and fifth each day) should consist of formula only. On a four-meal schedule, the first and fourth meals should be formula.

In either case, the second meal of the day should consist of chopped beef (preferably raw). The amount needed will vary from about three tablespoonfuls for Toy breeds up to one-half cupful for large breeds. The other meal should consist of equal parts of chopped beef and strained, cooked vegetables to which is added a little dry toast. (If you plan eventually to feed your dog canned food or dog meal, it can gradually be introduced at this meal.) Cod-liver oil and dicalcium phosphate should be mixed with the food for this meal. The amount of each will vary from one-half teaspoonful for Toys to 1 tablespoonful for large breeds.

The amount of food offered at each meal must gradually be increased and by five months the puppy will require about twice what he needed at three months. Puppies should be fat, and it is best to let them eat as much as they want at each meal, so long as they are hungry again when it is time for the next feeding. Any food not eaten within fifteen minutes should be taken away. With a little attention to the dog's eating habits, the owner can prepare enough food and still not waste any.

When the puppy is five months old, the final feeding of the day can be eliminated and the five meals compressed into four so the puppy still receives the same quantities and types of food. At six or seven months, the four meals can be compressed into three. By the time a puppy of small or medium breed is eleven to twelve months old, feedings can be reduced to two meals a day. At the end of the first year, cod-liver oil and dicalcium phosphate can usually be discontinued.

Large breeds mature more slowly and three meals a day are usually necessary until eighteen or twenty-four months of age. Cod-liver oil and dicalcium phosphate should be continued, too, until the large dog reaches maturity.

A mature dog usually eats slightly less than he did as a growing puppy. For mature dogs, one large meal a day is usually sufficient, although some owners prefer to give two meals. As long as the dog enjoys optimum health and is neither too fat nor too thin, the number of meals a day makes little difference.

The amount of food required for mature dogs will vary. With canned dog food or home-prepared foods (that is, the combination of meat, vegetables, and meal), the approximate amount required is one-half ounce of food per pound of body weight. Thus, about eight ounces of such foods would be needed each day for a mature dog weighing sixteen pounds. If the dog is fed a dehydrated commercial food, approximately one ounce of food is needed for each pound of body weight. Approximately one pound of dry food per day would be required by a dog weighing sixteen pounds. Most manufacturers of commercial foods provide information on packages as to approximate daily needs of various breeds.

As a dog becomes older and less active, he may become too fat. Or his appetite may decrease so he becomes too thin. It is necessary to adjust the diet in either case, for the dog will live longer and enjoy better health if he is maintained in trim condition. The simplest way to decrease or increase body weight is by decreasing or increasing the amount of fat in the diet. Protein content should be maintained at a high level throughout the dog's life, although the amount of food at each meal can be decreased if the dog becomes too fat.

If the older dog becomes reluctant to eat, it may be necessary to coax him with special food he normally relishes. Warming the food will increase its aroma and usually will help to entice the dog to eat. If he still refuses, rubbing some of the food on the dog's lips and gums may stimulate interest. It may be helpful also to offer food in smaller amounts and increase the number of meals per day. Foods that are highly nutritious and easily digested are especially desirable for older dogs. Small amounts of cooked, ground liver, cottage cheese, or mashed, hard-cooked eggs should be included in the diet often.

Before a bitch is bred, her owner should make sure that she is in optimum condition—slightly on the lean side rather than fat. The bitch in whelp is given much the same diet she was fed prior to breeding, with slight increases in amounts of meat, liver, and dairy products. Beginning about six weeks after breeding, she should be fed two meals per day rather than one, and the total daily intake increased. (Some bitches in whelp require as much as 50% more food than they consume normally.) She must not be permitted to become fat, for whelping problems are more likely to occur in overweight dogs. Cod-liver oil and dicalcium phosphate should be provided until after the puppies are weaned. The amount of each will vary from one-half teaspoonful to one tablespoonful a day, depending upon her size.

The dog used only occasionally for breeding will not require a special diet, but he should be well fed and maintained in optimum condition. A dog that is at public stud and used frequently may require a slightly increased amount of food. But his basic diet will require no change so long as his general health is good and his flesh is firm and hard.

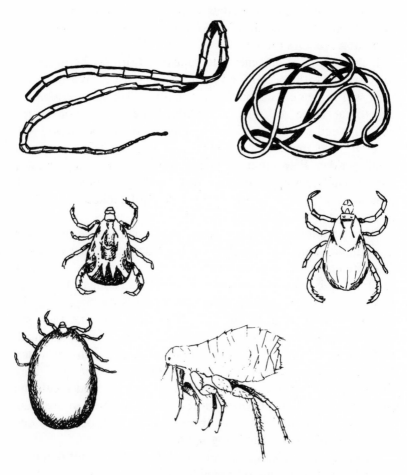

Some common internal and external parasites.

(UPPER LEFT) Tape worm. (UPPER RIGHT) Round worms. (CENTER) American dog ticks—left, female and right, male (much enlarged). (LOWER LEFT) Female tick engorged. (LOWER RIGHT) dog flea (much enlarged).

Maintaining the
Dog's Health

Proper nutrition is essential in maintaining the dog's resistance to infectious diseases, in reducing susceptibility to organic diseases, and, of course, in preventing dietary deficiency diseases.

Rickets is probably the most common deficiency disease and afflicts puppies not provided sufficient calcium and Vitamin D. Bones fail to calcify properly, development of teeth is retarded, joints become knobby and deformed, and muscles are flabby. Symptoms include lameness, arching of neck and back, and a tendency of the legs to bow. Treatment consists of providing adequate amounts of dicalcium phosphate and Vitamin D and exposing the dog to sunlight. If detected and treated before reaching an advanced stage, bone damage may be lessened somewhat, although it cannot be corrected completely.

Osteomalacia, similar to rickets, may occur in adult dogs. Treatment is the same as for rickets, but here, too, prevention is preferable to cure. Permanent deformities resulting from rickets or osteomalacia will not be inherited, so once victims recover, they can be used for breeding.

To prevent the growth of disease-producing bacteria and other micro-organisms, cleanliness is essential. All equipment, especially water and food dishes, must be kept immaculately clean. Cleanliness is also essential in controlling external parasites, which thrive in unsanitary surroundings.

Fleas, lice, mites, and ticks can be eradicated in the dog's quarters by regular use of one of the insecticide sprays with a four to six weeks' residual effect. Bedding, blankets, and pillows should be laundered frequently and treated with an insecticide containing rotenone or DDT. Treatment for external parasites varies, depending upon the parasite involved, but a number of good dips and powders are available at pet stores.

Fleas may be eliminated by using a flea powder containing lindane. The coat must be dusted thoroughly with the powder at frequent intervals during the summer months when fleas are a problem. For eradicating lice, dips containing rotenone or DDT must be applied to the coat. A fine-toothed comb should then be used to remove dead lice and eggs, which are firmly attached to the coat. Mites live deep in the ear canal, producing irritation to the lining of the ear and causing a brownish-black, dry type discharge. Plain mineral oil or ear ointment should be swabbed on the inner surface of the ear twice a week until mites are eliminated. Ticks may carry Rocky Mountain spotted fever, so, to avoid possible infection, they should be removed from the dog only with tweezers and should be destroyed by burning (or by dropping them into insecticide). Heavy infestation can be controlled by sponging the coat daily with a solution containing a special tick dip.

Among preparations available for controlling parasites on the dog's body are some that can be given internally. Since dosage must be carefully controlled, these preparations should not be used without consulting a veterinarian.

Internal parasites, with the exception of the tapeworm, may be transmitted from a mother dog to the puppies. Infestation may also result from contact with infected bedding or through access to a yard where an infected dog relieves himself. The types that may infest dogs are roundworms, whipworms, tapeworms, hookworms, and heartworms. All cause similar symptoms: a generally unthrifty appearance, stary coat, dull eyes, weakness and emaciation despite a ravenous appetite, coughing, vomiting, diarrhea, and sometimes bloody stools. Not all symptoms are present in every case, of course.

Promiscuous dosing for worms is dangerous and different types of worms require different treatment. So if you suspect your dog has worms, ask your veterinarian to make a microscopic examination of the feces, and to prescribe appropriate treatment if evidence of worm infestation is found.

Clogged anal glands cause intense discomfort, which the dog may attempt to relieve by scooting himself along the floor on his haunches. These glands, located on either side of the anus, secrete a substance that enables the dog to expel the contents of the rectum. If they become clogged, they may give the dog an unpleasant odor and when neglected, serious infection may result. Contents of the glands can be easily expelled into a wad of

cotton, which should be held under the tail with the left hand. Then, using the right hand, pressure should be exerted with the thumb on one side of the anus, the forefinger on the other. The normal secretion is brownish in color, with an unpleasant odor. The presence of blood or pus indicates infection and should be called to the attention of a veterinarian.

Fits, often considered a symptom of worms, may result from a variety of causes, including vitamin deficiencies, or playing to the point of exhaustion. A veterinarian should be consulted when a fit occurs, for it may be a symptom of serious illness.

Distemper takes many and varied forms, so it is sometimes difficult for even experienced veterinarians to diagnose. It is the number one killer of dogs, and although it is not unknown in older dogs, its victims are usually puppies. While some dogs do recover, permanent damage to the brain or nervous system is often sustained. Symptoms may include lethargy, diarrhea, vomiting, reduced appetite, cough, nasal discharge, inflammation of the eyes, and a rise in temperature. If distemper is suspected, a veterinarian must be consulted at once, for early treatment is essential. Effective preventive measures lie in inoculation. Shots for temporary immunity should be given all puppies within a few weeks after whelping, and the permanent inoculations should be given as soon thereafter as possible.

Hardpad has been fairly prevalent in Great Britain for a number of years, and its incidence in the United States is increasing. Symptoms are similar to those of distemper, but as the disease progresses, the pads of the feet harden and eventually peel. Chances of recovery are not favorable unless prompt veterinary care is secured.

Infectious hepatitis in dogs affects the liver, as does the human form, but apparently is not transmissible to man. Symptoms are similar to those of distemper, and the disease rapidly reaches the acute stage. Since hepatitis is often fatal, prompt veterinary treatment is essential. Effective vaccines are available and should be provided all puppies. A combination distemper-hepatitis vaccine is sometimes used.

Leptospirosis is caused by a micro-organism often transmitted by contact with rats, or by ingestion of food contaminated by rats. The disease can be transmitted to man, so anyone caring for an afflicted dog must take steps to avoid infection. Symptoms include vomiting, loss of appetite, diarrhea, fever, depression and lethargy, redness of eyes and gums, and sometimes jaundice. Since permanent kidney damage may result, veterinary treatment should be secured immediately.

Rabies is a disease that is always fatal—and it is transmissible to man. It is caused by a virus that attacks the nervous system and is present in the saliva of an infected animal. When an infected animal bites another, the virus is transmitted to the new victim. It may also enter the body through cuts and scratches that come in contact with saliva containing the virus.

All warm-blooded animals are subject to rabies and it may be transmitted by foxes, skunks, squirrels, horses, and cattle as well as dogs. Anyone bitten by a dog (or other animal) should see his physician immediately, and health and law enforcement officials should be notified. Also, if your dog is bitten by another animal, consult your veterinarian immediately.

In most areas, rabies shots are required by law. Even if not required, all dogs should be given anti-rabies vaccine, for it is an effective preventive measure.

Injuries of a serious nature—deep cuts, broken bones, severe burns, etc.—always require veterinary care. However, the dog may need first aid before being moved to a veterinary hospital.

A dog injured in any way should be approached cautiously, for reactions of a dog in pain are unpredictable and he may bite even a beloved master. A muzzle should always be applied before any attempt is made to move the dog or treat him in any way. The muzzle can be improvised from a strip of cloth, bandage, or even heavy cord, looped firmly around the dog's jaws and tied under the lower jaw. The ends should then be extended back of the neck and tied again so the loop around the jaws will stay in place.

A stretcher for moving a heavy dog can be improvised from a rug or board—preferably two people should be available to transport it. A small dog can be carried by one person simply by grasping the loose skin at the nape of the neck with one hand and placing the other hand under the dog's hips.

Severe bleeding from a leg can be controlled by applying a tourniquet between the wound and the body, but the tourniquet must be loosened at ten-minute intervals. Severe bleeding from head or body can be controlled by placing a cloth or gauze pad over the wound, then applying firm pressure with the hand.

To treat minor cuts, first trim the hair from around the wound, then wash the area with warm soapy water and apply a mild antiseptic such as tincture of metaphen.

Shock is usually the aftermath of severe injury and requires immediate veterinary attention. The dog appears dazed, lips and tongue are pale, and breathing is shallow. The dog should be wrapped in blankets and kept warm, and if possible, kept lying down with his head lower than his body.

Fractures require immediate professional attention. A broken bone should be immobilized while the dog is transported to the veterinarian but no attempt should be made to splint it.

Burns from hot liquid or hot metals should be treated by applying a bland ointment, provided the burned area is small. Burns over large areas should be treated by a veterinarian.

Burns from chemicals should first be treated by flushing the coat with plain water, taking care to protect the dog's eyes and ears. A baking soda solution can then be applied to neutralize the chemical further. If the burned area is small, a bland ointment should be applied. If the burned area is large, more extensive treatment will be required, as well as veterinary care.

49

Poisoning is more often accidental than deliberate, but whic[.] ever the case, symptoms and treatment are the same. If the poisoning is not discovered immediately, the dog may be found unconscious. His mouth will be slimy, he will tremble, have difficulty breathing, and possibly go into convulsions. Veterinary treatment must be secured immediately.

If you find the dog eating something you know to be poisonous, induce vomiting immediately by repeatedly forcing the dog to swallow a mixture of equal parts of hydrogen peroxide and water. Delay of even a few minutes may result in death. When the contents of the stomach have been emptied, force the dog to swallow raw egg white, which will slow absorption of the poison. Then call the veterinarian. Provide him with information as to the type of poison, and follow his advice as to further treatment.

Some chemicals are toxic even though not swallowed, so before using a product, make sure it can be used safely around pets.

Electric shock usually results because an owner negligently leaves an electric cord exposed where the dog can chew on it. If possible, disconnect the cord before touching the dog. Otherwise, yank the cord from the dog's mouth so you will not receive a shock when you try to help him. If the dog is unconscious, artificial respiration and stimulants will be required, so a veterinarian should be consulted at once.

Eye problems of a minor nature—redness or occasional discharge—may be treated with a few drops of boric acid solution (2%) or salt solution (1 teaspoonful table salt to 1 pint sterile water). Cuts on the eyeball, bruises close to the eyes, or persistent discharge shoud be treated only by a veterinarian.

Skin problems usually cause persistent itching. However, *follicular mange* does not usually do so but is evidenced by moth-eaten-looking patches, especially about the head and along the back. *Sarcoptic mange* produces severe itching and is evidenced by patchy, crusty areas on body, legs, and abdomen. Any evidence suggesting either should be called to the attention of a veterinarian. Both require extensive treatment and both may be contracted by humans.

Eczema is characterized by extreme itching, redness of the skin and exudation of serous matter. It may result from a variety of causes, and the exact cause in a particular case may be difficult to determine. Relief may be secured by dusting the dog twice a week with a soothing powder containing a fungicide and an insecticide.

Allergies are not readily distinguished from other skin troubles except through laboratory tests. However, dog owners should be alert to the fact that straw, shavings, or newspapers used for bedding, various coat dressings and shampoos, or simply bathing the dog too often, may produce allergic skin reactions in some dogs. Thus, a change in dog-keeping practices often relieves them.

Symptoms of illness may be so obvious there is no question that the dog is ill, or so subtle that the owner isn't sure whether there is a change from normal or not. *Loss of appetite, malaise* (general lack of interest in what is going on), *and vomiting* may be ignored if they occur singly and persist only for a day. However, in combination with other evidence of illness, such symptoms may be significant and the dog should be watched closely. *Abnormal bowel movements,* especially diarrhea or bloody stools, are cause for immediate concern. *Urinary abnormalities* may indicate infections, and bloody urine is always an indication of a serious condition. When a dog that has long been housebroken suddenly becomes incontinent, a veterinarian should be consulted, for he may be able to suggest treatment or medication that will be helpful.

Persistent coughing is often considered a symptom of worms, but may also indicate heart trouble—especially in older dogs.

Vomiting is another symptom often attributed to worm infestation. Dogs suffering from indigestion sometimes eat grass, apparently to induce vomiting and relieve discomfort.

Stary coat—dull and lackluster—indicates generally poor health and possible worm infestation. *Dull eyes* may result from similar conditions. Certain forms of blindness may also cause the eyes to lose the sparkle of vibrant good health.

Fever is a positive indication of illness and consistent deviation from the normal temperature range of 100 to 102 degrees is cause for concern. To take the dog's temperature, first place the dog on his side. Coat the bulb of a rectal thermometer with petroleum jelly, raise the dog's tail, insert the thermometer to approximately

51

half its length, and hold it in position for two minutes. Clean the thermometer with rubbing alcohol after each use and be sure to shake it down.

A dog that is seriously ill, requiring surgical treatment, transfusions, or intravenous feeding, must be hospitalized. One requiring less complicated treatment is better cared for at home, but it is essential that the dog be kept in a quiet environment. Preferably, his bed should be in a room apart from family activity, yet close at hand, so his condition can be checked frequently. Clean bedding and adequate warmth are essential, as are a constant supply of fresh, cool water, and foods to tempt the appetite.

Special equipment is not ordinarily needed, but the following items will be useful in caring for a sick dog, as well as in giving first aid for injuries:

petroleum jelly	tincture of metaphen
rubbing alcohol	cotton, gauze, and adhesive tape
mineral oil	burn ointment
rectal thermometer	tweezers
hydrogen peroxide	boric acid solution (2%)

If special medication is prescribed, it may be administered in any one of several ways. A pill or small capsule may be concealed in a small piece of meat, which the dog will usually swallow with no problem. A large capsule may be given by holding the dog's mouth open, inserting the capsule as far as possible down the throat, then holding the mouth closed until the dog swallows. Liquid medicine should be measured into a small bottle or test tube. Then, if the corner of the dog's lip is pulled out while the head is tilted upward, the liquid can be poured between the lips and teeth, a small amount at a time. If he refuses to swallow, keeping the dog's head tilted and stroking his throat will usually induce swallowing.

Foods offered the sick dog should be particularly nutritious and easily digested. Meals should be smaller than usual and offered at more frequent intervals. If the dog is reluctant to eat, offer food he particularly likes and warm it slightly to increase aroma and thus make it more tempting.

Housing Your Dog

Every dog should have a bed of his own, snug and warm, where he can retire undisturbed when he wishes to nap. And, especially with a small puppy, it is desirable to have the bed arranged so the dog can be securely confined at times, safe and contented. If the puppy is taught early in life to stay quietly in his box at night, or when the family is out, the habit will carry over into adulthood and will benefit both dog and master.

The dog should never be banished to a damp, cold basement, but should be quartered in an out-of-the-way corner close to the center of family activity. His bed can be an elaborate cushioned affair with electric warming pad, or simply a rectangular wooden box or heavy paper carton, cushioned with a clean cotton rug or towel. Actually, the latter is ideal for a new puppy, for it is snug, easy to clean, and expendable. A "door" can be cut on one side of the box for easy access, but it should be placed in such a way that the dog can still be confined when desirable.

The shipping crates used by professional handlers at dog shows make ideal indoor quarters. They are lightweight but strong, provide adequate air circulation, yet are snug and warm and easily cleaned. For the dog owner who takes his dog along when he travels, a dog crate is ideal, for the dog will willingly stay in his accustomed bed during long automobile trips, and the crate can be taken inside motels or hotels at night, making the dog a far more acceptable guest.

Dog crates are made of chromed metal or wood, and some have tops covered with a special rubber matting so they can be used as grooming tables. Anyone moderately handy with tools can construct a crate similar to the one illustrated on page 35.

Crates come in various sizes, to suit various breeds of dogs. For reasons of economy, the size selected for a puppy should be adequate for use when the dog is full grown. If the area seems too large when the puppy is small, a temporary cardboard partition can be installed to limit the area he occupies.

The dog owner who lives in the suburbs or in the country may want to keep a mature dog outdoors part of the time, in which case an outdoor doghouse should be provided. This type of kennel can also be constructed by the home handyman, but must be more substantial than quarters used indoors.

Outside finish of the doghouse can be of any type, but double wall construction will make for greater warmth in chilly weather. The floor should be smooth and easy to clean, so tongued and grooved boards or plywood are best. To keep the floor from contact with the damp earth, supports should be laid flat on the ground, running lengthwise of the structure. 2 x 4s serve well as supports for doghouses for small or medium breeds, but 4 x 4s should be used for large breeds.

The outdoor kennel must be big enough so that the dog can turn around inside, but small enough so that his body heat will keep it warm in chilly weather. The overall length of the kennel shoud be twice the length of the adult dog, measured from tip of nose to onset of tail. Width of the structure should be approximately three-fourths the length. And height from the floor to the point where the roof begins should be approximately one and a half the adult dog's height at the shoulders. If you build the house when the dog is still a puppy, you can determine his approximate adult size by referring to the Standard for his breed.

An "A" type roof is preferable, and an overhang of six inches all the way around will provide protection from sun and rain. If the roof is hinged to fold back, the interior of the kennel can be cleaned readily.

The entrance should be placed to one side rather than in the center, which will provide further protection against the weather. One of the commercially made door closures of rubber will keep out rain, snow, and wind, yet give the pet complete freedom to enter and leave his home.

The best location for the doghouse is where it will get enough morning sun to keep it dry, yet will not be in full sun during hot afternoons. If possible, the back of the doghouse should be placed toward the prevailing winds.

A fenced run or yard is essential to the outdoor kennel, and the fence must be sturdy enough that the dog cannot break through it, and high enough so he cannot jump or climb over it. The gate should have a latch of a type that can't be opened accidentally. The area enclosed must provide the dog with space to exercise freely, or else the dog must be exercised on the leash every day, for no dog should be confined to a tiny yard day after day without adequate exercise.

The yard must be kept clean and odor free, and the doghouse must be scrubbed and disinfected at frequent intervals. One of the insecticides made especially for use in kennels—one with a four to six weeks' residual effect—should be used regularly on floors and walls, inside and out.

Enough bedding must be provided so the dog can snuggle into it and keep warm in chilly weather. Bedding should either be of a type that is inexpensive, so it can be discarded and replaced frequently, or of a type that can be laundered readily. Dogs are often allergic to fungi found on straw, hay, or grass, and sometimes newspaper ink, but cedar shavings and old cotton rugs and blankets usually serve very well.

The Stone-age Dog

A Spotted Dog from India, "Parent of the Modern Coach dog."

History of
the Genus Canis

The history of man's association with the dog is a fascinating one, extending into the past at least seventy centuries, and involving the entire history of civilized man from the early Stone Age to the present.

The dog, technically a member of the genus *Canis,* belongs to the zoological family group *Canidae,* which also includes such animals as wolves, foxes, jackals, and coyotes. In the past it was generally agreed that the dog resulted from the crossing of various members of the family *Canidae.* Recent findings have amended this theory somewhat, and most authorities now feel the jackal probably has no direct relationship with the dog. Some believe dogs are descended from wolves and foxes, with the wolf the main progenitor. As evidence, they cite the fact that the teeth of the wolf are identical in every detail with those of the dog, whereas the teeth of the jackal are totally different.

Still other authorities insist that the dog always has existed as a separate and distinct animal. This group admits that it is possible for a dog to mate with a fox, coyote, or wolf, but points out that the resulting puppies are unable to breed with each other, although they can breed with stock of the same genus as either parent. Therefore, they insist, it was impossible for a new and distinct genus to have developed from such crossings. They then cite the fact that any dog can be mated with any other dog and the progeny bred among themselves. These researchers point out, too, heritable characteristics that are totally different in the three animals. For instance, the pupil of the dog's eye is round, that of the wolf oblique, and that of the jackal vertical. Tails, too, differ considerably, for tails of foxes, coyotes, and wolves always drop behind them, while those of dogs may be carried over the back or straight up.

Much conjecture centers on two wild dog species that still exist—the Dingo of Australia, and the Dhole in India. Similar in appearance, both are reddish in color, both have rather long,

57

slender jaws, both have rounded ears that stand straight up, and both species hunt in packs. Evidence indicates that they had the same ancestors. Yet, today, they live in areas that are more than 4,000 miles apart.

Despite the fact that it is impossible to determine just when the dog first appeared as a distinct species, archeologists have found definite proof that the dog was the first animal domesticated by man. When man lived by tracking, trapping, and killing game, the dog added to the forces through which man discovered and captured the quarry. Man shared his primitive living quarters with the dog, and the two together devoured the prey. Thus, each helped to sustain the life of the other. The dog assisted man, too, by defending the campsite against marauders. As man gradually became civilized, the dog's usefulness was extended to guarding the other animals man domesticated, and, even before the wheel was invented, the dog served as a beast of burden. In fact, archeological findings show that aboriginal peoples of Switzerland and Ireland used the dog for such purposes long before they learned to till the soil.

Cave drawings from the palaeolithic era, which was the earliest part of the Old World Stone Age, include hunting scenes in which a rough, canine-like form is shown alongside huntsmen. One of these drawings is believed to be 50,000 years old, and gives credence to the theory that all dogs are descended from a primitive type ancestor that was neither fox nor wolf.

Archeological findings show that Europeans of the New Stone Age possessed a breed of dogs of wolf-like appearance, and a similar breed has been traced through the successive Bronze Age and Iron Age. Accurate details are not available, though, as to the external appearance of domesticated dogs prior to historic times (roughly four to five thousand years ago).

Early records in Chaldean and Egyptian tombs show that several distinct and well-established dog types had been developed by about 3700 B.C. Similar records show that the early people of the Nile Valley regarded the dog as a god, often burying it as a mummy in special cemeteries and mourning its death.

Some of the early Egyptian dogs had been given names, such as Akna, Tarn, and Abu, and slender dogs of the Greyhound type and a short-legged Terrier type are depicted in drawings found

Bas-relief of Hunters with Nets and Mastiffs. From the walls of Assurbanipal's palace at Nineveh 668-626 B.C. *British Museum.*

in Egyptian royal tombs that are at least 5,000 years old. The Afghan Hound and the Saluki are shown in drawings of only slightly later times. Another type of ancient Egyptian dog was much heavier and more powerful, with short coat and massive head. These probably hunted by scent, as did still another type of Egyptian dog that had a thick furry coat, a tail curled almost flat over the back, and erect "prick" ears.

Early Romans and Greeks mentioned their dogs often in literature, and both made distinctions between those that hunted by sight and those that hunted by scent. The Romans' canine classifications were similar to those we use now. In addition to dogs comparable to the Greek sight and scent hounds, the ancient Romans had Canes *villatici* (housedogs) and Canes *pastorales* (sheepdogs), corresponding to our present-day working dogs.

The dog is mentioned many times in the Old Testament. The first reference, in Genesis, leads some Biblical scholars to assert that man and dog have been companions from the time man was created. And later Biblical references bring an awareness of the diversity in breeds and types existing thousands of years ago.

As civilization advanced, man found new uses for dogs. Some required great size and strength. Others needed less of these characteristics but greater agility and better sight. Still others needed an accentuated sense of smell. As time went on, men kept those puppies that suited specific purposes especially well and bred them together. Through ensuing generations of selective breeding, desirable characteristics appeared with increasing frequency. Dogs used in a particular region for a special purpose gradually became more like each other, yet less like dogs of other areas used for different purposes. Thus were established the foundations for the various breeds we have today.

The American Kennel Club, the leading dog organization in the United States, divides the various breeds into six "Groups," based on similarity of purposes for which they were developed.

"Sporting Dogs" include the Pointers, Setters, Spaniels, and Retrievers that were developed by sportsmen interested in hunting game birds. Most of the Pointers and Setters are of comparatively recent origin. Their development parallels the development of sporting firearms, and most of them evolved in the British Isles. Exceptions are the Weimaraner, which was developed in Germany, and the Vizsla, or Hungarian Pointer, believed to have been developed by the Magyar hordes that swarmed over Central Europe a thousand years ago. The Irish were among the first to use Spaniels, though the name indicates that the original stock may have come from Spain. Two Sporting breeds, the American Water Spaniel, and the Chesapeake Bay Retriever, were developed entirely in the United States.

"Hounds," among which are Dachshunds, Beagles, Bassets, Harriers, and Foxhounds, are used singly, in pairs, or in packs to "course" (or run) and hunt for rabbits, foxes, and various rodents. But little larger, the Norwegian Elkhound is used in its native country to hunt big game—moose, bear, and deer.

The smaller Hound breeds hunt by scent, while the Irish Wolfhound, Borzoi, Scottish Deerhound, Saluki, and Greyhound hunt by sight. The Whippet, Saluki, and Greyhound are notably fleet of foot, and racing these breeds (particularly the Greyhound) is popular sport.

The Bloodhound is a member of the Hound Group that is known world-wide for its scenting ability. On the other hand, the Basenji is a comparatively rare Hound breed and has the distinction of being the only dog that cannot bark.

"Working Dogs" have the greatest utilitarian value of all modern dogs and contribute to man's welfare in diverse ways. The Boxer, Doberman Pinscher, Rottweiler, German Shepherd, Great Dane, and Giant Schnauzer are often trained to serve as sentries and aid police in patrolling streets. The German Shepherd is especially noted as a guide dog for the blind. The Collie, the various breeds of Sheepdogs, and the two Corgi breeds are known throughout the world for their extraordinary herding ability. And the exploits of the St. Bernard and Newfoundland are legendary, their records for saving lives unsurpassed.

The Siberian Husky and the Alaskan Malamute are noted for tremendous strength and stamina. Had it not been for these hardy Northern breeds, the great polar expeditions might never have taken place, for Admiral Byrd used these dogs to reach points inaccessible by other means. Even today, with our jet-age transportation, the Northern breeds provide a more practical means of travel in frigid areas than do modern machines.

"Terriers" derive their name from the Latin *terra,* meaning

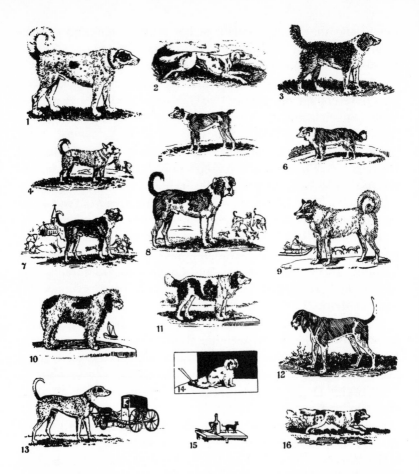

1. The Newfoundland. 2. The English Setter. 3. The Large Water-spaniel. 4. The Terrier. 5. The Cur-dog. 6. The Shepherd's Dog. 7. The Bulldog. 8. The Mastiff. 9. The Greenland Dog. 10. The Rought Water-dog. 11. The Small Water-spaniel. 12. The Old English Hound. 13. The Dalmatian or Coach-dog. 14. The Comporter (very much of a Papillon). 15. "Toy Dog, Bottle, Glass, and Pipe." *From a vignette.* 16. The Springer or Cocker. *From Thomas Bewick's "General History of Quadrupeds" (1790).*

"earth," for all of the breeds in this Group are fond of burrowing. Terriers hunt by digging into the earth to rout rodents and fur-bearing animals such as badgers, woodchucks, and otters. Some breeds are expected merely to force the animals from their dens in order that the hunter can complete the capture. Others are expected to find and destroy the prey, either on the surface or under the ground.

Terriers come in a wide variety of sizes, ranging from such large breeds as the Airedale and Kerry Blue to such small ones as the Skye, the Dandie Dinmont, the West Highland White, and the Scottish Terrier. England, Ireland, and Scotland produced most of the Terrier breeds, although the Miniature Schnauzer was developed in Germany.

"Toys," as the term indicates, are small breeds. Although they make little claim to usefulness other than as ideal housepets, Toy dogs develop as much protective instinct as do larger breeds and serve effectively in warning of the approach of strangers.

Origins of the Toys are varied. The Pekingese was developed as the royal dog of China more than two thousand years before the birth of Christ. The Chihuahua, smallest of the Toys, originated in Mexico and is believed to be a descendant of the Techichi, a dog of great religious significance to the Aztecs, while the Italian Greyhound was popular in the days of ancient Pompeii.

"Non-Sporting Dogs" include a number of popular breeds of varying ancestry. The Standard and Miniature Poodles were developed in France for the purpose of retrieving game from water. The Bulldog originated in Great Britain and was bred for the purpose of "baiting" bulls. The Chowchow apparently originated centuries ago in China, for it is pictured in a bas relief dated to the Han dynasty of about 150 B.C.

The Dalmatian served as a carriage dog in Dalmatia, protecting travelers in bandit-infested regions. The Keeshond, recognized as the national dog of Holland, is believed to have originated in the Arctic or possibly the Sub-Arctic. The Schipperke, sometimes erroneously described as a Dutch dog, originated in the Flemish provinces of Belgium. And the Lhasa Apso came from Tibet, where it is known as "Abso Seng Kye," the "Bark Lion Sentinel Dog."

During the thousands of years that man and dog have been closely associated, a strong affinity has been built up between the two. The dog has more than earned his way as a helper, and his faithful, selfless devotion to man is legendary. The ways in which the dog has proved his intelligence, his courage, and his dependability in situations of stress are amply recorded in the countless tales of canine heroism that highlight the pages of history, both past and present.

Dogs in Woodcuts. (*1st row*) (LEFT) "Maltese dog with shorter hair"; (RIGHT) "Spotted sporting dog trained to catch game"; (*2nd row*) (LEFT) Sporting white dog; (RIGHT) "Spanish dog with floppy ears": (*3rd row*) (LEFT) "French dog"; (RIGHT) "Mad dog of Grevinus"; (*4th row*) (LEFT) Hairy Maltese dog; (RIGHT) "English fighting dog . . . of horrid aspect." *From Aldrovandus (1637).*

Early History of the Basenji

How old is the Basenji breed? Where did it originate? Some historians have placed the Basenji as far back as Biblical days—a theory yet unproven. What is established is that evidences of a dog closely resembling the Basenji have been identified in excavations of ancient Egyptian tombs, in drawings on walls, in friezes, and on various ornamental objects such as urns and bowls found in burial chambers. It is evident that the dog played a vital role in the lives of the Egyptians and was revered and cherished by them. Hieroglyphs and drawings by early Egyptians depict the curly tailed dog with foxy ears along with birds, fish, horses, cattle, antelope, and giraffes. There is definite proof that the Basenji did exist as early as 3,000 B.C.

A magnificent limestone statue of a dog, dating to the Sixteenth Dynasty, is in the Louvre Museum in Paris. A bell of fine rope hangs from the neck of the dog, which appears to be a Basenji. If it is, this statue would date the breed as far back as 1,600 B.C.

It has been established that the Basenji is unaltered from its original type and remains the same as when first rediscovered by explorers in Africa in the late nineteenth century. Depending upon the locale, the dogs were given varying names—Congo Terriers, Bongo Dogs, Nyam Nyam, or Zande. One explorer in Central Africa describes the canines as being of a wolf-type with curly tails and having short coats of a yellowish tan with a white stripe around the neck. Wooden bells were strapped to the loins of these barkless dogs to provide a means of locating them during hunting forays.

The Basenjis first introduced to the Western World came from the area along the upper reaches of the Congo River in the Eastern Belgian Congo, from Southern Sudan, and from the area north of Leopoldville inhabited by the Nyam Nyam tribes.

Later, Basenjis were found in Liberia and Rhodesia. However, by that time, explorers, missionaries, and representatives of Western business corporations had come into the territory. They had brought dogs with them and the native dogs, including Basenjis, were bred with them. Delightful as is the barkless nature of the Basenji to civilized man, the natives had not found it an asset, especially for hunting purposes, since the lack of a bark made it more difficult to locate the dogs when they spotted game. It was mainly the missionaries and the plantation operators sent to Africa by foreign businesses who became interested in retaining the purebred native Basenji. It was they who established the selective breeding programs and continued them over a period of years.

The first Basenjis to be seen outside their native land were two dogs, referred to as African Bush Dogs or Congo Terriers, which were shown at England's Crufts Dog Show in 1895. These two were purchased by Mr. W. E. Temple and Mr. H. C. Brooks, both authorities on foreign dogs. Unfortunately the pair died of distemper shortly after the Crufts Show. About this same time, a pair was reported seen in Paris, and, later, at the turn of the century, a Congo bitch and her daughter were photographed at the Berlin Zoo in Germany.

In a book published by H. A. Graaf von Bylandt in 1904, two pictures of typical Basenjis owned by a Mr. L'Hoest of Anvers, Belgium, were included. On another page was a photograph of one owned by the Zoological Garden of Paris. All were called Congo Terriers. In another book by the same author and published by Les Races de Chiens in 1897, there is a drawing of a group of four dogs. The inscription under the drawing identifies the dogs as being from the Sandeh or Zande country.

Many theories have been presented to explain the barkless nature of the Basenji. One was that the dog had been trained not to bark, probably to make him a silent hunting dog. A rather ridiculous conjecture was that a curse had been put upon the breed in ancient times as punishment for some misdemeanor. Neither theory is acceptable to modern, scientific man. It was Retired Army Captain F. B. Johnson who eventually found the answer—one verified as medical fact. Captain Johnson has recorded his findings in his book, *Basenji—Dog From The Past*. It is with his permission that I relate the account of his research.

To some people it was mystifying that upon occasion, especially if the dog was startled, he would make a sound resembling an abortive bark. He also made other noises unlike those heard in any other breed. Captain Johnson decided that he needed the larynx of one or more deceased Basenjis to determine whether there was a physiological or a structural reason for the Basenji's inability to bark.

Miss Phyliss Elliott of Malta, Illinois, one of this country's early breeders, lost two beloved Basenjis simultaneously, but, knowing of Captain Johnson's research, she laid aside her heartbreak and had her veterinarian remove the larynges from the dogs.

Dr. Erwin Small, professor of Veterinary Clinical Medicine, and Dr. L. E. St. Clair, professor of Biological Structure, of the College of

Fula of the Congo—a "legend in her time," brought from her native Africa by Miss Veronica Tudor-Williams.

Veterinary Medicine at the University of Illinois, agreed to make the examination. They reported their findings as follows:

"We have examined the larynx of the Basenji and compared it with a normal dog and cow. The following is a report of our findings. The vocal folds and muscles do not appear different. The ventricle has a position as usual except that it is very shallow. This prevents the vocal fold from being free on its lateral side. Apparently, this limits the vibrations of the vocal fold. In the cow, there is no ventricle and no prominent vocal fold."

This, then, is the medical explanation. The Basenji cannot bark because the physical structure of the larynx differs from that of other canines. However, this does not prevent his making other vocal sounds.

Ch. Mymaron Rain-gauge.

Ridingold Sir Buntar of Horsley.

International Ch. Azenda Sweet Conclusion of Dormtiki.

The Breed in England

In 1923, Lady Helen Nutting, a devotee of the Basenji, attempted to establish the breed in England. On a trip to the Zande, she made arrangements with Major L. N. Brown to bring six Basenjis back with her to England, but, while still in quarantine, the dogs died as the result of distemper inoculation.

It is to Mrs. Olivia Burn that credit must be given for successfully launching the Basenji in England. As a result of her efforts, the breed was recognized and accepted for registration in England. However, this was not accomplished without a great deal of heartbreak. Of the five Basenjis Mrs. Burn brought back on her first trip to Africa, only one little bitch survived the immunization against distemper. Mrs. Burn kept her as a pet.

In 1933, after much persuasion, Mrs. Burn obtained a dog from a chief of the Feshis. Kiluba came safely through quarantine and the little bitch was mated to him, but a freak accident during the mating caused an infection which resulted in her death.

Returning to the Congo, Mrs. Burn brought back to England two dogs that were registered with her Blean Kennel name. They were Bongo of Blean and Bokoto of Blean. Mr. Forest N. Hall, noted American Basenji breeder and all-breed judge, says that in his opinion Bongo was the greatest Basenji of his day. Certainly his progeny are indicative of the accuracy of Mr. Hall's opinion.

Mrs. Burn, in the June 1937 issue of the *American Kennel Gazette*, stated that her dogs came from the Belgian Congo, and continued, "the best ones on the plateau among the warlike or hunting tribes of Bapedni. . . . These dogs are indigenous to the vast areas of Central Africa. Mainly in the interior. Some from the Nyam Nyam and Manboutu tribes are thicker and shorter on the leg, but they are used by the hungry as a table delicacy."

It was not until 1939 that Miss Veronica Tudor-Williams was able to gratify her desire for a Basenji, but her luck was like that of Mrs. Burn in this first effort. The beautiful little bitch, which came from the Sudanese natives, arrived safely in England but soon after arriving in quarantine died of rabies from a bite received prior to leaving the Sudan. A year later, Miss Tudor-Williams successfully imported a tri-color dog and a red and white bitch from the

Sudan-Yganda border. The little bitch proved an unsatisfactory breeding specimen, so a pet home was found for her. The male, Simolo, was retained as an outcross dog.

It was through the generosity of Mr. and Mrs. Arthur Byron that Miss Tudor-Williams obtained the little bitch Amatangazig, who was to be the foundation bitch of breedings in both England and America. Zig came from the Sudan and was brought to England by the Byrons. It is said that it was Zig who contributed to the English Basenjis the short backs and soundness combined with daintiness.

The year 1947 brought the first English Basenji champions—litter brother and sister Ch. Fern of the Congo and Ch. Brown Trout of the Congo, grandchildren of Zig. They also had the distinction of being the first tri-color Basenjis on the Continent.

In 1959, Miss Tudor-Williams returned from the Congo with the red and white bitch whose destiny it was to contribute more to the breed, perhaps, than any Basenji in the world. This was Fula of the Congo. Fula has been called a "legend in her time," and no more fitting tribute could be paid this great little Basenji.

Among early breeders whose dogs are found in international pedigrees is Mrs. E. G. Anderson, whose Andersley breeding has been the foundation of prominent kennels throughout the world. Others are Mrs. L. R. Percival of the Littlebreach Basenjis and the R. J. Williamses of the Syngefield Basenjis. These breeders produced such famous ones as Ch. Andersley Atlantic, Ch. Bianca of Littlebreach, Ch. Ravenhead Barnaby of Littlebreach, Ch. Leda of Syngefield, and Ch. Syngefield Leonata of Littlebreach.

Miss Phyliss M. Cook's Riviana Basenjis, dating back to early English stock, are still producing winners—an outstanding one being Ch. Riviana Kingfisher.

The Ridingold Kennels of Mrs. Cecil Tress gained repute with such notables as Ch. Ridingold Fantasia and, later, Ridingold's Sir Bunter of Horsley, who, combined with Horsley stock, produced some of the world's outstanding black and white Basenjis.

Miss Diana Berry's Ch. Hobby Horse of Sin is an outstanding example of her Sin breeding and the many others coming before and after him.

Mrs. Bunty Bowers' Domewood Kennels gave to the breed such champions as Ch. The Ardent Wooer of Domewood, Ch. Sindy of Horsley, and, more currently, Ch. Domewood Gainesborough Lady.

The Drumadoon Basenjis of Mrs. Margot Bowden, formerly of

International Ch. Arabella
Azenda.

Riviana Black Ivory.

Ch. Hobby Horse of Sin.

International Ch. Azenda Ful-of-It, bred by Miss Phyliss M. Cook, England, and owned by Miss Karen Wallinder, Sweden.

England but now in Canada, have had a strong influence throughout England, Canada, and the United States. American and Canadian Ch. Drumadoon Dresden is noted for her contributions to the breed.

Mr. Fred Jones, Joyfred Basenjis, not only has shown his dogs to championship but also has brought the breed to prominence in the sports field through his interest in hunting with Basenjis.

Miss Margaret Christy-Davies' Azenda breeding continued to produce champions of international fame. Among them are International Ch. Azenda Ful-Of-It, International Ch. Arabella Azenda, and International Ch. Azenda Sweet Conclusion of Dormtiki.

From the Dormtiki Kennels of Mrs. C. W. White comes Ch. Fula Zig Zag of the Congo. Another of her Basenjis, from a breeding combining the bloodlines of Azenda and Dormtiki, was sold to Miss Karin Wallinder of Gothenberg, Sweden. This dog, International Ch. Azenda Sweet Conclusion of Dormtiki, was awarded Best in Show in 1975, competing in an entry of 1,400 all-breed dogs to attain this top honor.

Ch. White Wood Christmas Bell, bred by Miss Diane Berry, England.

Mrs. A. E. Cardew, St. Erme Basenjis, bred the famed Ch. St. Erme Fula Falcon as well as two of the 1975 Top Basenjis of England. They are Ch. St. Erme Dancing Kestral and Ch. St. Erme Dancing Eagle.

In the Horsley Kennels of Commander and Mrs. Patrick Stringer were bred such notables as Ch. Sir Ceciltar of Horsley, Ch. Serendatar of Horsley, and Ch. Sir Casper of Horsley.

Other breeders in England who have made outstanding contributions are the Misses Juniper, Mr. J. Fleming, Mrs. E. M. Ford, Mr. Jack Malcolm, the Fields of Houndsmark, Mr. Ben Johnson, Mrs. C. M. Graham, and Mrs. M. A. Brown.

The 1975 Top Basenjis of England are Ch. Colonel Phaeton of Courtland, Ch. Niangara Klipspringer, Ch. St. Erme Dancing Kestral, Ch. Domewood Funny Girl, Ch. Riviana Kingfisher, Ch. St. Erme Dancing Eagle, Tinkis Titans Trottie True, Ch. Domewood Double Diamond, Ch. Horsleys Sir Prydeau, Ch. Fula Zig Zag of the Congo, and Ch. Domewood Gainesborough Lady.

St. Erme Fula Falcon of the Congo.

Canadian, Bermudian, American Ch. Pyramid's Zulu, owned by Harry and Violette Lazarenko, Canada.

Ch. Fula Princess of the Congo, bred by Miss Veronica Tudor-Williams and owned by Malcolm McDonald, Canada.

Basenjis in Canada

In 1940, the late Dr. A. R. B. Richmond of Toronto, Ontario, Canada, imported four Basenjis from the Of the Congo Kennels of Miss Veronica Tudor-Williams. They were to provide the foundation for the Basenjis of North America. The two males were Kwillo of the Congo and Koodoo of the Congo; the females were Kikuyu of the Congo and Kitieve of the Congo.

Next came such prominent breeders as Mrs. J. W. (Sheila) Anderson of Victoria, British Columbia, and Mrs. Roberta Jenkins of Toronto, Ontario. Mrs. Anderson's Glenairley Kennel produced some of North America's outstanding champions. Her Canadian Ch. Joss of Glenairley, C.D., was the first Basenji to qualify for championship and an obedience degree. Mrs. Anderson was also responsible for providing some of the dogs used in the James Street movie *Goodbye My Lady* and acted as a consultant on the set when the picture was being made. One of the Basenjis used as a "stand in" was Ch. Flageolet of the Congo, who was later purchased by Norm and Mae Wallace of Tinas Coma Kennels in Burlington, Washington.

Mrs. Jenkins' Blue Nile Basenjis produced the first Basenji to win a Group in Canada. This was Canadian and American Ch. Abakaru of the Blue Nile, who was also the first to attain both Canadian and American titles.

Mrs. Margaret Bowden was the breeder of the storied Canadian and American Ch. Dainty Dancer of Glenairley. Dainty, when only four weeks and five days old, was sold to Mrs. Margaret Robertson, also of Victoria, and became the foundation bitch for her Merlea Kennels. Shown in September 1957 at the Vancouver Island Dog Fanciers Show, Dainty was awarded Best in Show, Best Canadian Bred, and Best Canadian Bred Puppy. In October of the same year, she again went Best in Show, and she finished her championship in the spring of 1958 with yet another Best-in-Show win.

Dainty was shown in Seattle, Washington, in February 1958, where she gained her first five American points and won the Hound Group. Winning repeatedly in both the United States and Canada, Dainty never failed to place in the Group when she was the breed

Ch. Coco of the Congo, grandson of Amatanazig, native African dog bred by Miss Veronica Tudor-Williams, owned by the late George L. Gilkey, United States foundation breeder.

Canadian and American Ch. Dainty Dancer of Glenairley.

winner. Perhaps her most spectacular win was at the Renton, Washington, Kennel Club Show in 1958 when she took Best in Show in a six-hundred forty-dog entry. Dainty's spectacular wins merited her the Canadian Kennel Club medal as the top winning dog of any breed in Canada, the Ken-L Ration award for the top winning dog of all breeds of the Western area, and the BCOA Hound Group Trophy once and their Best-in-Show Trophy for two consecutive years. Dainty was Best in Show seven times at all-breed shows in Canada and the United States. Her picture was

Canadian and American Ch. Benji Tricop Golden Deor, bred and owned by Malcolm McDonald. Listed in Top Winning Canadian Dogs of 1972.

designated to be used on the Basenji Club of Canada letterhead as the club's insignia.

In later years there were two Best-in-Show Basenji wins in Canada. Ch. Spearwood Tirzah, owned by Mrs. Cheryl Myers, Minto, New Brunswick, went Best in Show as a puppy in 1973. Later, another Basenji puppy, Carina's Christmas Ginger Snap, bred by Mrs. Charon Rolls of Pasadena, Newfoundland, was awarded Best in Show.

The first Canadian Basenji Specialty Championship Show was held at Saint John, New Brunswick, in August 1967. The winner was a tri-color puppy, Benji Tricop Ebony Kayunga, who was later to attain both his championship and the C.D. degree. His breeder was Malcolm McDonald, a notable breeder of long standing whose current winning dog is American and Canadian Ch. Benji Tricop Golden Deot, a litter brother of Ch. Benji Tricop Ebony Kayunga, C.D.

The outstanding Pyramid Basenjis of Mr. and Mrs. Harry Lazarenko of Willow Lake, Ontario, include Canadian, American, and Bermudian Ch. Pyramid's Zulu of Zanzu. "Dr. Zu" went Best Puppy in Show at his first show at six months, and, while still entered in the Puppy Class, he was awarded Best of Breed at the 1969 Basenji Club of Canada Specialty over forty-three Class entries and eighteen Specials.

Zulu continued his glamorous show career in 1970 with nine Group placements and twenty-eight Best-of-Breed wins, which included the Breed win at a Basenji Club of America Specialty. The same year Zulu gained his Bermudian title by winning three majors over top American and Bermudian entries on a four-day Bermuda circuit.

Zulu's American championship was climaxed with two Best-of-Breed wins in 1971. With limited showing, Zulu was third winning Basenji in Canada in 1972. He has sired eleven champions.

Pyramid Kennels has attained C.D. degrees on two of their champions—Ch. Pyramid's Enchantress, C.D., and Pyramid's Kayzu, C.D. They have been awarded Best Brace in Show twice.

American and Canadian Ch. Katanga's War Lord of Bomar, owned by Diane Vievira of Weston, Ontario, and Dr. and Mrs. Martin Abelson of Harrison, New York, was the first black and white to win championships in the two countries. Ch. Gamble Bi-Golly of Bomar, owned by the Martin Harrisons, was the first black and white bitch to gain her championship first in Canada and then in the United States.

Ch. Betsy Ross Kingola of Ber Vic.

Ch. Kasha's Brave Bantu of Anubis.

Ch. Sirius Halfback.

The Basenji's Debut in the United States

September 1977 will mark the fortieth anniversary of the Basenji's debut in the United States. Arriving on the S. S. Barengaria with Mr. and Mrs. Byron Rogers of New York City in September 1937 were three Basenjis the couple had acquired in England. The event was perpetuated by a feature in *Life Magazine*. The two bitches, Bereke of Blean and Bokoto of Blean, were bred by the English pioneer of the breed, Mrs. Olivia Burn. The male, imported by Mrs. Burn from Africa and still in quarantine when the Rogers purchased him, was Bakuma of Blean, bred by the Chief of Donkesse and whelped in July 1936.

The two bitches, sired by Mrs. Burn's famed Bongo of Blean, were not destined to make a contribution to the establishment of the breed in this country. They died within a year of their arrival. The male, Bakuma of Blean, or Boyce as he was called by the Rogers, was lost sight of for a time after being sold to a pet home. It was not until after 1940, when the Alexander Phemisters, foundation breeders of the United States, purchased their first Basenjis, that it was resolved that the dog they knew as Wallop or Bois was in reality, Bakuma of Blean.

In actuality, the Rogers' three Basenjis were not the first to arrive in this country, although they were the first live specimens. On July 20, 1912, Explorers Lang and Chapin, returning from an expedition to Garamba in the Belgian Congo, brought with them a mounted male Basenji which today can be seen in the reproduction of a Pygmy village in the Museum of Natural History in New York City.

Before Bois was to make his contribution to the breed, a little stowaway bitch arrived in Boston on April 13, 1941, aboard the freighter West Leshaway, which was returning from a West African port. Apparently having fallen down the hold of the ship while it was being loaded, the little bitch was not discovered until the ship docked in Boston. Half-starved, dehydrated, and in emotional shock from the traumatic voyage, she was a pitiful sight. She was turned over to the Boston Animal League and the resulting publicity brought Alexander Phemister onto the scene. He convinced the League that the dog was a Basenji and that he was

79

knowledgeable of the breed. Following a period of rehabilitation at the Animal League, the little bitch was released into the custody of the Phemisters. She was registered as Phemister's Congo and became their foundation Basenji.

In August 1941, Congo was sent to Canada to be bred to Dr. A. R. B. Richmond's Koodoo of the Congo. Three puppies came from this mating—a bitch, Phemister's Naida, and two males, Phemister's Bwana and Phemister's Barrie. Barrie was the first Basenji in the United States to attain the C.D.X. degree. He was later sold to Mrs. John Taaffee of California.

Meanwhile, in the fall of 1941, a hunting expedition from Leopoldville, the Belgian Congo, landed in New York with a consignment of eight gorillas for Mr. Henry A. Trefflich, an importer of mammals, birds, and reptiles. It has been said that Basenjis were caged with the gorillas and that the gorillas were playing with them and tossing them from one to another like toys. Mr. Trefflich showed a pair of the Basenjis at the 1941 Madison Square Garden Show for "exhibition only." Then called Congo and Libra, they were purchased by Mrs. John Taaffee and registered as Kindu and Kasenyi.

Basenjis were introduced pictorially in the 1938 Westminster catalog. Olga and Byron Rogers bought a full page ad in the catalog inviting the public to a display of the Barkless Basenjis at Dogs, Inc., 59 East 52nd Street, New York City. The photograph in the ad showed a pair of very handsome Basenjis.

The Basenji made its show debut in the United States on May 31, 1941, at Morris and Essex. No further details were obtainable.

The year 1943 recorded the first entry of Basenjis at the Westminster Kennel Club Show, where two were entered in the Miscellaneous Class—Koodo of the Congo, bred by Miss Veronica Tudor-Williams, and Juliana of Windrush, bred by Dr. A. R. B. Richmond. Both were owned by the Phemisters. Koodoo placed first in Miscellaneous Dogs and Juliana was first in Bitches. The breed name in the catalog was misspelled "Besenjis"!

It was not until November 9, 1943, that the breed was recognized by The American Kennel Club. The June 1944 *Stud Book* lists the names of the first thirty-nine Basenjis registered. The one-hundred mark required for Group classification was not attained until 1945, when 106 Basenjis were recorded. The breed was then placed in the Hound Group.

In February 1945, the late Alva Rosenberg judged Basenjis at Westminster while they were still entered in the Miscellaneous

Jadi's Akida, first home-bred champion of Jadi Basenjis, Mrs. Peggie C. Peek.

Ch. Foxkin Sun Imp Ti-Habib, owned by Bob and Ann Lee.

Ch. Khajah's Gay Excalibur, bred by Mrs. Shirley Chambers. One of the Top Ten Breed and Group Winners, 1974-77.

Ch. Cambria's Nyakatii, bred and owned by Robert J. Mankey. First Basenji to place at Westminster and Best of Breed in 1966 and 1967.

Ch. Benji Tricop Ebony Kayunga, C.D., bred and owned by Malcolm McDonald, Canada.

Ch. Rangi's Black Amon, bred and owned by Forrest and Lou Dye.

Ch. Makila Motane Moke, owned by Michael Work.

Ch. Tinas Coma Mumbo Jumbo, bred by Norm and Mae Wallace and owned by Charles E. and Ouida McGahee.

Class. He placed the dogs as follows: First, Kindu (African-bred), owned by Mrs. John Taaffee; Second, Phemister's Kamante (Phemister's Bois x Juliana of Windrush), bred and owned by the Alexander Phemisters; and Third, Zippi of the Congo (Kinga of the Congo x Amatangazig), bred by Miss Veronica Tudor-Williams and owned by George L. Gilkey. Bitch placements were: First, Thurza of Windrush (Ch. Kwillo of the Congo x Kikuyu of the Congo), bred by Dr. A. R. B. Richmond and owned by Mary Mc-Wain; and Fourth, Mofwe (Jinga x Rosemary of Windrush), bred by Dr. Eloise Gerry and owned by Dr. Carsten Johnson.

It was the year 1946! Basenjis were dignified on this momentous occasion by being entered in the Hound Group at Westminster, enabling them to compete for championship points. The placements by Judge Anton A. Rost were: American-bred Dogs and Bitches—First, Mofwe's Zimba (Phemister's Bois x Mofwe), owned and bred by Carsten Johnson; and Second, Kano of Rhosenji (Pistol Pete x Tanya of Windrush), bred by George L. Gilkey and owned by Carsten Johnson. Winners in Open Dogs and Bitches were Phemister's Kenga (Phemister's Berecke, C.D., x Phemister's Makima), owned by R. P. Valtier. Best of Winners was Mofwe's Zimba, and Best of Breed was Ch. Phemister's Melengo (Phemister's Bois x Zinnia of the Congo), owned by Mr. and Mrs. Phemister. Melengo was the first Basenji champion in the United States.

At the 1947 Westminster Show, Mr. Rosenberg again judged Basenjis. There were three Specials in the competition and Ch. Phemister's Melengo won Best of Breed for the second consecutive year. Best of Opposite Sex was Ch. Haku Kimbu (Phemister's Bois x Bobo of Windrush), bred by Mary McWain and owned by Andrew J. McWain.

By the time of the 1950 Westminster Show, Judge Forest N. Hall, Hallwyre Kennels of Dallas, Texas, had made his spectacular entry into the world of Basenjis with Ch. Kingolo, a foundation dog by Kindu x Kasenyi. Even as his sons were following in his famous footsteps, Kingolo was "packing his trunk" for a move to Ireland, to the R. J. Williams' home. Shown twelve times in the United States, Kingolo was awarded Best of Breed at Westminster in 1948 by Judge Louis J. Murr and again in 1949 by Judge William Kendrick. Kingolo placed Second in the Group twice, Fourth twice, and was undefeated in the Classes during his brief show career in this country. Kingolo sired six champions before his departure to Ireland. His notable offspring in the United Kingdom included Ch. Andersley Atlantic, Ch. Andersley Americana, Ch. Jamy of Littlebreach, Ch. Jessica of Littlebreach, Ch. Syngefield Leonato of Littlebreach, Ch. Pongo of the Congo, Ch. Petal of the Congo, Ch. Victory of Syngefield, and Ch. Leda of Syngefield. The latter was purchased by the late Bettina Belmont Ward, thus bringing Kingolo's bloodlines combined with the English, back to the United States.

Kingolo's notable progeny in the United States, prior to his departure for Ireland, included Ch. Kingolo's Kontender, sire of Ch. Phemister's Kedar, who was among the foundation stock for Robert J. Mankey's Cambria Kennels. Another outstanding Kingolo son was Ch. Kingolo's Kan Kan, who completed his championship in three five-point shows.

Another Kingolo son, Kingolo's Korporal, was Winners Dog at the 1950 Westminster Show, and Ch. Kingolo's Kan Kan was Best of Breed under Judge Lewis S. Worden. Mr. Forest Hall was owner of both dogs. There was an entry of seven at the show.

With seven Basenjis entered at the 1951 Westminster Show and two absentees, Judge Chris Shuttleworth awarded Best of Winners to Tanca Mu Jungle Jonny (Ch. Faithhaven Biagukin x Ch. Skreets of the Fires), a dog bred and owned by Mrs. Mabell Cadwell. Best of Opposite Sex was Ch. Black Mist of the Congo, bred by Veronica Tudor-Williams and owned by Mary McWain, one of the first tri-colors to be imported to the United States. Best of Breed was Ch. Phemister's Maestro, bred and owned by the Phemisters.

Four of the five entries were shown at the 1952 Westminster Show, with Best of Breed going to Mary McWain's tri-color Ch. Haku Black Icicle. Winners Dog was Phemister's Sandoa. There were no bitches entered. Mr. Walter H. Reeves judged.

Judge Percy Roberts gave Miss McWain's Ch. Black Ace of the Congo, another tri-color, Best of Breed at the 1953 Westminster Show, and Phemister's Sandoa, Winners Dog. Winners Bitch, Best of Winners, and Best of Opposite Sex was Fairmont Lynn Lysande, bred and owned by Mrs. Evan A. T. Westlin. Miss McWain was the first United States breeder to import tri-colors, and her Ch. Black Mist of the Congo was the first Basenji to win the Hound Group.

Counting the Westminster Show of 1954, Basenjis were entered in 379 shows from 1949 to 1954.

According to the records of George Gilkey, Mary and Alexander Phemister were responsible for getting the Basenji Club of America off to an early start. There was much preliminary work to be ac-

Ch. Kukuk's Harvey Wallbanger, bred and owned by Mr. and Mrs. H. W. Kukuk.

Ch. Khajah's Gay Tamara, bred by Mrs. Shirley Chambers and owned by Mrs. William F. Davis.

Ch. The Phantom of Omar, owned by Mrs. Patrina Black, Omar Basenjis.

Ch. Tar's Black Jack of Omar, bred by Mrs. Sandra M. Lewis and owned by Mrs. Patrina Black and Chris Johnson, Omar Basenjis.

Ch. Philo's Blaze of Ko Ko Krater, first Basenji to go Best in Show in the United States. Bred by Mr. and Mrs. Lyle Vaughn and owned by Lieutenant and Mrs. Albert Ashurst.

Ch. Shikari's Zuri, bred and owned by Mrs. Patricia Church. A consistent winner on the West Coast.

Green Acre's Nellie Forbush, left, and Caucasian King of the Congo, right, foundation stock for Mrs. Marion R. Mangrum's Caucasian Kennels. Bred by Hugh L. and Evelyn M. Green.

Khani's Questt O'Candida, owned by Robert Frost and Mrs. Virginia O'Connor, Hawaii.

complished before the Basenji was recognized by The American Kennel Club, and the Phemisters did much of this groundwork.

Following recognition, the first Basenji to be shown as a member of the Hound Group was Binji, owned by F. Kyle of California. Since there was only one entry, no points were earned. It is interesting to note, however, that Binji later became a champion and at the time he was finished, he was carrying Mr. Kyle's kennel prefix, Koh I Noor.

The history of the foundation breeders would be incomplete without more detailed mention of George L. Gilkey. His dedication to the breed, his interest in its promotion, and his meticulous recording of the breed's early history in this country are ample evidence of his devotion to the breed. Foundation bitch for Mr. Gilkey's Rhosenji Kennels was Tanya of Windrush, whom he purchased in June 1941 from Dr. A. R. B. Richmond. Champions accredited to Rhosenji are Ch. Coco of the Congo, bred by Veronica Tudor-Williams, Ch. Keta of Rhosenji, Ch. Rho of Rhosenji, Ch. Rhosenji's Beau, Ch. Rosenji's Ginger, and Ch. Kan of Basen-Box. Ch. Rhosenji's Beau's colorful show ring career included his defeat of eleven other Basenji champions and being awarded Best of Breed at the first Basenji Specialty in the United States when his litter sister Ch. Rhosenji's Ginger was awarded Best of Opposite Sex.

An outstanding father-son breeder combination was Ralph and Joe Lepper of Indianapolis, Indiana. Their Ch. Lepper's Nik Nak was a two-time Best-in-Show winner and was Number One in the Top Ten Breed Winners with twenty-four wins. Their English and American Ch. Andersley Amazala contributed much to the breed through his progeny. Other notables owned by the Leppers were Ch. Lepper's Blackberry, Ch. Lepper's Red Pepper, Ch. Chico of the Congo, Ch. Lepper's Red Fury, and Ch. Lepper's Dark Town Strutter.

The first point-winning Basenjis were shown at the Vancouver (Washington) Kennel Club Show on July 15, 1945. Mr. H. N. Francis of How Gert Kennels, Portland, Oregon, entered six dogs and six bitches and put five points on the dog and five on the bitch. Best of Breed was Andy of Glen Ho, whom Francis had purchased from Homer Garland. Francis' bitch winner, Twanda, whom he had bought from BCOA charter member Dr. Eloise Gerry, was Best of Opposite Sex.

On August 25, 1945, the Phemisters entered five Basenjis at the North Shore Kennel Club Show at Hamilton, Massachusetts. Best of Breed went to Ch. Zinnia of the Congo, a daughter of the African import Amatangazig and a litter mate of Zippi of the Congo and Zeppo of the Congo. Best of Opposite Sex was Phemister's Simba, sired by Phemister's Bois x Zinnia of the Congo.

The first Basenji Specialty was held on June 11, 1950, at Batavia, New York, with Alva Rosenberg judging. Twenty dogs from seven states competed. Best of Breed was Rhosenji's Beau, and Best of Opposite Sex was his litter sister Rhosenji's Ginger.

The second Specialty was held on September 9, 1951, at the Westchester Kennel Club Show, with Dr. Mitten judging the entry of forty Basenjis. Phemister's Maestro went Best of Breed with Phemister's Gold Charmer as Best of Opposite Sex.

At the third Specialty, held on September 5, 1952, Best of Breed was Ch. Vagabond of the Congo, owned by Leon Shadic, and Best of Opposite Sex was the Phemister's Katema of Carmel. Mr. E. H. Lounsbury judged the entry of twenty-seven.

Beginning in 1959, three BCOA regional specialties were held yearly. The first (Mid-West) was in Louisville, Kentucky, on March 1, 1959, with an entry of twenty-three. Breed winner was Miacor's Zuchil and Best of Opposite Sex was Pampei of Curli Tail. Next was the Western Specialty held on July sixteenth at Santa Barbara, California, with an entry of eighty-three. Best of Breed was Bettina's Oribi and Best of Opposite Sex was Cambria's Taboo. Third was the Eastern Specialty, held on December fifth at Philadelphia, Pennsylvania, with twenty-three dogs competing. Bettina's Oribi was Best of Breed and Bettina's Vita was Best of Opposite Sex. Both were bred and owned by Bettina Belmont Ward.

It was not until the early sixties that black and white Basenjis were introduced into the United States. Their origin, as with the more typical red and whites and tri-colors, is African.

The first known black and white to be whelped in this country, although not eligible for registration by The American Kennel Club, was Black Diamond of Cyron (Miliku). Her dam, Kiki of Cyron, was bred in Liberia and brought to this country by Dr. and Mrs. Leon Standifer. Her sire was registered by the A.K.C., but her dam's Kennel Union of South Africa registration was not acceptable to the A.K.C. The Standifers were living in Baton Rouge, Louisiana, when Kiki's litter was whelped. Miliku was obtained from them by Mrs. Shirley Chambers of Khajah Kennels, Reg., but she could not breed Miliku because she was unable to register her. The African ancestry behind Kiki of Cyron is re-

Ch. Bazimba's
Most Happy Fella.

Brabar's Barintha.

Ch. Black Power of
Woz.

Sudan Senji.

Ch. Gary Dee Super Star.

Ch. Kenara's En-
chanted Fox.

Ch. Reveille Ruffles of Rose Bay.

Congoglen Brianna.

Ch. Glenairley Black Munia.

English and American Ch. Andersley Amazala.

Ch. Sir Datar of Horsley.

Ch. Bettina's Oribi.

corded in the March-April 1964 issue of the BCOA *Bulletin,* as re-lated by Dr. Standifer, who was stationed for two years (1959-1960) at the Firestone Plantation in Liberia.

Other black and whites were discovered in Rhodesia by missionaries or in white settlements where breeding programs similar to that at Firestone were followed—selective breeding programs such as those used the world over. Many Basenjis from these breedings have attained Kennel Union of South Africa championships and are accepted for registration in England but not by The American Kennel Club.

The first black and white to be registered in this country is said to have been Khajah's Black Fula Challenge (Fula Reveille of the Congo x Fulaflashi of the Congo). Probably the first black and white to earn an obedience degree was Khaja's Black Jack, C.D., bred by Mrs. Shirley Chambers and owned by George and Jane Larsen.

In 1962, Mrs. Gwen Stanich of Coptokin Kennels in South Elgin, Illinois, a subscriber to the English publication *Our Dogs,* saw show results from the Kennel Union of South Africa. She noted a black and white Basenji, Taysenji Dopa, listed among the winners. Hoping to preserve the pure black and white color, obviously rare in the breed, Mrs. Stanich wrote the KUSA for further information.

A year later, Mrs. Stanich sent two red and white bitches to Mrs. E. M. Ford in Zambia, North Rhodesia. They were Coptokin Bikini and Coptokin Beautique. Beautique was bred to Taysenji Tigee and shipped to England, where she whelped a litter of three while still in quarantine. The litter was registered by the Kennel Club of Great Britain. The black and white male, Taysenji Kwidi, and the bitch, Taysenji Bwenu, were sent to Mrs. Stanich. The red and white bitch, Taysenji Twuy, remained in England.

Coptokin Copper Bikini was bred to KUSA Ch. Lazi of the Senjis. Bikini had already won her KUSA championship, too, the first United States-bred Basenji to attain an African title. The five black and white puppies from Bikini's litter by Lazi arrived in this country in 1966. They were Coptokin Amerique, Coptokin Ameliana, Coptokin Africana, Coptokin Americana, and Coptokin Atlantic—of the Senjis. Three of these bitches, Ameliana, Americana, and Amerique were bred to their grandsire on their dam's side, English and American Ch. Andersley Atlantic. Ameliana was the first to whelp in this country—producing two reds, two tricolors, and one black and white male who was A.K.C.

registered Coptokin The Black Ashanti. He is owned and has been shown by Basenji Breeder-Judge John Loukota of Ingleside, Illinois.

Notable among present-day black and whites are Ch. Kasha's Cominique of Anubus, bred by Mrs. Pat Ringle; Ch. Datar of Horsley, bred by Horsley Kennels of England and owned by Mrs. Shirley Chambers; Ch. Horsley's Sir Frobishertar, bred by Horsely Kennels and owned by Mrs. Pat Church; Ch. Black Power of Woz, bred by the Land of Woz Basenjis and owned by Mrs. Carol Shubert; and Ch. Bushveld Black Shikari, owned by Mrs. Roberta Fredrick and the first black and white Group winner bred in this country.

The years 1965 to 1976 are proof that Basenjis have come a long way since their recognition by the A.K.C. in 1943. Breed winners at Westminster for these years are: 1965, Ch. Feruzi of the Zande (Ross and Betsy Newmann); 1966, Cambria's Nyakatii (Robert J. Mankey), also placed Fourth in the Group; 1967, a repeat— Cambria's Nyakatii, this time placing Second in the Group; 1968, Cambria's Zoleka (Robert Mankey), placed Second in the Group; 1969, Ch. Betsy Ross Kingola of Ber Vic (Betsy and Ross Newmann), placed Fourth in the Group; 1970, Ch. Reveille Re-Up (Mrs. Elaine Hoffmann); 1971 Ch. Reveille Re-Up, placed Second in the Group; 1972, Ch. Reveille Re-Up, placed First in the Group; 1973, Ch. Reveille Be Sirius (Mr. and Mrs. J. H. Symington); 1974, Ch. Reveille Be Sirius, placed Fourth in the Group; 1975, Ch. Libra's Apollo of Delahi (Robert J. Mankey); and 1976, Ch. Kopper Karisimbi of the Nile (Mrs. M. R. Setzer). It is noteworthy that all the above winners were owner-handled other than Reveille Re-Up and Reveille Be Sirius, who were handled by their breeder, Miss Damara Bolté.

Looking back to the outstanding Group and Breed winners from the years 1954 to 1957 are notables whose progeny are represented in the great champions and producers of today: 1954-55, Ch. Phemister's Kedar and Ch. Ponjol of Tan-Ca-Mu; 1956, Ch. Brahme of Syngefield and the first Best-in-Show winner, Philo's Blaze of Ko Ko Krater; and 1957, Best-in-Show winner Ch. Dainty Dancer of Glenairley and Breed winner Ch. Bettina's Ferret.

Later, in 1965, the top Breed winner was Cambria's Shar. Other top winners were Ch. Khaja's Gay Fula Cadet, Ch. Cambria's Bwasisi, Ch. Ketket's Night Lightening, and Ch. Cambria's Nyakatii. In 1966 top winners were Ch. Gay Fula Cadet, Ch. Cambria's Garvin, Ch. Reveille Rebel, and Ch. Peregrine of Ros-

Jadi's Black Javelin.

Ch. Cambria's Ti-Zar.

Ch. Lepper's Nik Nak.

Ch. Cambria's Ti Mungai.

Ch. Kukuk's Gay Apollo, C.D.

Ch. Il-Se-Ott Golden Majorette, U.D.T.

Ch. Uhuru Avalanche of Woz.

Ch. Sirius Scarlet O'Hara.

Kindu and Kasenyi, imported with shipment of gorillas for Mr. Henry A. Trefflich.

Coco of the Congo.

Ch. Sirius Flanker.

Ch. Reveille Recruit.

santy. In 1967 top winners were Ch. Cambria's Nyakatii again, Ch. Gay Fula Cadet, Ch. Reveille Re-Up, Ch. Blythe of Dell, and Ch. Gay Cadet of Woz. Winners in 1968 were Ch. Gay Fula Cadet (top Breed winner), Ch. Adam of Eterndo, Ch. Cambria's Nyakatii, Ch. Shangu of Hills Half Acre, and Betsy Ross Top Kick of Dhajo.

Top breed winners for 1969 were Ch. Betsy Ross Kingola of Ber Vic, Ch. Shangu of Hills Half Acre, Ch. Red Man of Rancho Rest, Ch. Khajah's Gay Flambeau of Ed-Jo, and Ch. Fula Danzon of the Congo. The 1970 winners were Ch. Betsy Ross Golden Jet, Ch. Reveille Re-Up, Ch. Shangu of Hills Half Acre, Ch. Tejay's Anubus, and Ch. Sirius Halfback. In 1971 top winners were Ch. Luddymarie Betsy Ross Melissa, Ch. Woodlyn Hegemony of Woz, Ch. Phemister Happy Day, Ch. Tanda's Pagan Baron, Ch. Reveille Re-Up, Ch. Sirius Halfback, Ch. Rujak's Golden Hagigi, Ch. Darp's Re-Up of Sowega, and Ch. Lihu's D'Dugu of Flambeau.

In 1972 there were such top winners as Ch. Africaner Boog a Loo, Ch. Reveille Be Sirius, Ch. Rewald's Ebenezer, Ch. Arisongo's Zrus, Ch. Black Power of Woz, Ch. Betsy Ross Joyful Saint, Ch. Makila Curtain Call, Ch. Shetari's Teddy Bear, and Ch. Shadowbye's Mitty.

In 1974 leading winners were Ch. Shadowbye's Mitty, Ch. Black Power of Woz, Ch. Khajah's Gay Excalibur, Ch. Reveille Be Sirius, Ch. Betsy Ross Barki Serengeti, Ch. Kasha's Brave Bantu of Anubis, Ch. Betsy Ross Joyful Saint, Ch. Gary Dee's Super Star, and Ch. Libra's Apollo of Delahi.

Among the great ones to be remembered for their continuing contribution to the breed through their progeny are: Ch. Cambria's Ti-Mungai, Ch. Flageolet of the Congo, Ch. Brahme of Syngefield, Ch. Lepper's Mr. Spats, Ch. Rivianna Jasper Lad, Ch. Bettina's Oryx, Ch. Fulahill of the Congo, Ch. Tinas Mumbo Jumbo, Ch. Phemister's Keda, Ch. Reveille Recruit, Ch. Reveille Ruffles of Rose Bay, Ch. Fulafaun of the Congo, Ch. Khajah's Gay Fula Cadet, Ch. Cambria's Bwasisi, Ch. Reveille Rebel, Ch. Redwing of Rancho Rest, Ch. Fulaflashi of the Congo, American and Canadian Ch. Tinas Coma Ouimac A-Okay, Ch. Peregrine of Rossanty, and Ch. Luddymarie's Merry Mad Cap.

The history of the Basenji in the United States would be incomplete without a special section devoted to the contribution Hawaii has made to the breed. Kindu and Kasenyi were the foundation stock. Mrs. Helene (Lyle) Vaughn of Ko Ko Krater Kennels in Honolulu brought the famed pair to the Islands. Mr. and Mrs.

Vaughn had made a trip to California for the express purpose of purchasing two Doberman Pinschers. They contacted Mrs. John Taaffee, who was closing her kennel following the death of her husband. It was there they met and fell in love with Kindu and Kasenyi. The Vaughns promptly bought the pair for the sum of $300.00, a great bargain—so they thought! And it would have been, had there not been an additional $300.00 board bill for the required one-hundred-twenty-day quarantine period upon their return to Honolulu.

Hawaii gave this country the first Best-in-Show Basenji: Philo's Blaze of Ko Ko Krater, bred by the Vaughns and owned by Lieutenant and Mrs. Albert Ashurst. This event took place at the Maui Kennel Club Show on October 13, 1956. The handler was Lyle Vaughn and the Judge was Forest N. Hall.

Another early winner from the Ko Ko Krater Kennels was Kindulu. Judge Forest Hall gave him Best of Breed at the Maui Kennel Club Show on October 12, 1952, and placed him Second in the Hound Group. Also, Best of Breed, Best of Winners, Best of Opposite Sex, and Third in the Group for a four-point win at the Hawaiian Kennel Club Show on April 28, 1957, was Vagabond of Ko Ko Krater with Mr. Albert Van Court judging.

A second Best-in-Show award for a Basenji was scored in Hawaii in 1962 when Judge William J. Fox awarded the top honor to Pharoah's Prince Kimpoko at the Hawaiian Kennel Club's Labor Day Show.

Another champion of note in the late sixties was Ch. Keiki O Ka Amka Po, bred by Terry L. and Virginia Ellis, and co-owned by Frank M. Angell and the late Dorothy Gowen, one of Hawaii's foundation breeders. Winning his first major at the Maui Kennel Club Show in May 1967, he was also placed First in the Hound Group by Judge Vincent G. Perry. When Keiki was awarded his second major under Judge R. W. Cross, he was also given Best of Breed and placed Second in the Hound Group under Mrs. Helen Walsh.

The one-hundred-twenty-day quarantine period has presented a grave obstacle to Hawaiian breeders acquiring dogs from "the outside." Two breeders have been the main contributors to Hawaiian bloodlines—Miss Veronica Tudor-Williams and Mrs. Connie Britton.

The Basenji Club of Hawaii, Inc., and its dedicated members have made great strides in the two years since its incorporation. Now included in the club's activities are educational programs, handling classes for juniors and breed clubs, and obedience training. Rex Tanaka is largely responsible for the latter. He has ably proven his abilities in the field of obedience training with the accomplishments of his own Basenji, Ch. Il-Se-Ott Golden Majorette (Tammy), who achieved the U.D.T. degree. In 1969, she was the third highest scoring C.D. in the nation; in 1971, she was awarded highest average score in Open competing for her C.D.X.; in 1972, Tammy acquired her T.D. degree, making her the first and only Tracking Basenji; in 1973, she received the highest single score in Utility; and in 1974, she completed her Utility degree. In 1971 and 1972, Tammy was given recognition in *Front and Finish Magazine* as one of the outstanding Basenjis in obedience work.

Other Basenjis in Hawaii that have earned obedience degrees are: Pharoah's Pride, C.D., owned by Karen Arakaki; Fula Fair Lady of the Congo, C.D., owned by Rex Tanaka; and Tenkis Fula Aquarius Azenda, C.D.X., owned by P. K. and D. Juniper.

One of the outstanding accomplishments of the Hawaiian breeders and the ultimate proof of their dedication to the breed is the program they have initiated for the control and eventual elimination of hemolytic anemia in Basenjis. This was one of the first breed clubs to engage in a cooperative effort to collect blood samples to test for the presence of the disease. Engaging the services of a veterinarian to draw the samples, breeders brought their dogs to a central station at an appointed time, and sent the samples in a single shipment to the testing center. When test results were obtained, a selective breeding program was adopted which would ensure against propagation of the disease.

Ch. Phemister's Simba.   Ch. Kingolo's Kontender.

89

Ch. Domewood The Artful Dodger, bred by Mrs. Bunty Bowers of England and owned by Mrs. Doreen Duffin of Australia.

Australian Basenjis

In 1948, the late Dr. Lex Caselberg and his wife of Wollogon, New South Wales, decided to import a harlequin Great Dane from England to their Danecourt Kennels. With the purchase of Repose of the Wideskies came a Great Dane breeder's handbook. Used as a marker in the book was a clipping of Dane news from one of the English dog journals. The clipping dropped on the floor one evening when Dr. Caselberg was browsing through the book. As he retrieved it, he glanced casually at the item on the reverse side of the clipping. It was about the Barkless Dog of the Congo. The Caselbergs were so fascinated with the content of the article that they promptly decided to import a pair. In mid-1948, Fanfare of the Congo and Cocotte of the Congo arrived from Miss Veronica Tudor-Williams, shortly to be followed by Andersley Aurora. On November first, Fanfare and Cocotte produced the first Basenji litter whelped in Australia.

Along with the Caselbergs, Mr. Mike Thomas, Mrs. Cormack, and Mr. and Mrs. Lloyd were among the early prominent breeders. All went well until the late fifties when ill health forced Dr. Caselberg to forego his involvement with dogs, and other breeders followed him. In the mid-sixties there came imports from New Zealand—mainly from the kennels of Clendo and Jordone—and the breed was given a boost. Prominent breeders at this time were Mrs. Hancock of New South Wales; Genoa Kennels in Ballarat, Victoria; Mrs. Kneip in New South Wales; Mrs. P. Forster in Victoria; and Mrs. L. Barker in Victoria.

The first Basenji club in Australia—the Basenji Club of Victoria—was formed by Mrs. Barker. Another followed shortly after in New South Wales. Recently clubs have been organized in Western and South Australia.

Basenjis from England and New Zealand, and one from America, have contributed to the Australian kennels. A recent import was Ch. Domewood Artful Dodger, bred by Mrs. Bunty Bowers of England. Mr. and Mrs. Duffin had the thrill of seeing "Artie" win Best Exhibit in Hound Group at his first show, only four days after his release from three months' quarantine. In two months of being shown, Artie amassed the one hundred points required for championship status in Australia and was never beaten in his class. He then achieved the distinction of being proclaimed Best in Show at the Victoria Kennel Club All Breed Show on October 4, 1975—the first Basenji in that area to win that top award. The Duffin's Ch. Panderville's Dinkle Doll was brought from England in 1973.

In Carlingford, New South Wales, the Keith Jordans race, hunt, and show their Congoglen Basenjis. Notable among them was Ch. Congobell Nutmeg, winner of many Challenge Certificates and Best-of-Breed awards and acknowledged as one of the top brood bitches in Australia. The Jordan's Wandra Belinda, a flashy tri-color, has won several Challenge Certificates and Best-of-Breed awards and was also named the Top Racing Bitch in New South Wales.

Other leading kennels in New South Wales are the Abada Kennels of Mr. and Mrs. F. Anderson and the Pukkanaut Kennels of Mr. and Mrs. A. Hunt.

In Victoria are such well-known breeders as Mrs. L. Barker, Wandra Kennels; Mr. and Mrs. R. Harper, Pharaoh Kennels; Mrs. E. Canavan, Azande Kennels; and Mr. and Mrs. Duffin, Makuba Kennels.

International Ch. Tauny Simba, imported to France from England by Mrs. Mavis-Barbara Rundle.

The Breed in France

Not until 1974 was the Basenji Club de France granted affiliation with the *Societe Centrale Canine,* with Monsieur Jean Servier as the club's founder-president and Mrs. Mavis-Barbara Rundle as *presidente d' honneur,* when Her Serene Highness the Princess Antionette of Monaco accepted the club under her patronage. The Princess has been a long-time devotee of Basenjis and is the owner of two Alverne Basenjis—The Laughing Water D'Alverne and her litter sister The Whispering Wind D'Alverne. Two Basenji Specials were promptly organized following the founding of the club, the first of which was at Cambria, where nine Basenjis were entered. Winners at this historic event were: Dog—CACIB and CAC—Ici Tobi D'Alverne, bred by Mrs. Rundle and owned by Madame Helene Josson, club vice-president; Reserve Dog—Voila Mister Speaker D'Alverne, bred by Mrs. Rundle and owned by Madame Desschans; and Bitches—CACIB and CAC—Voila La Speakerine D'Alverne, bred by Mrs. Rundle and owned by Madame Desschans.

An accomplishment of great significance to the breed was the establishment in 1974 of the Scientific Genetic Research Centre for Basenjis in France. The Centre is under the direction of Mrs. Rundle and under the control of Dr. Daniel Vallon of Antibes, the club geneticist. The founding of this research institute is a boon to Basenjis world-wide, since it has the advantage of being able to study with minute precision all of the French-bred Basenjis from their foundation stock to the present day.

In June 1974, the World Championship Show was held in Paris. There was an entry of fourteen dogs. Titles were awarded to: Dog, Vizir D'Iwor D'Antep, bred by Mella Castanier and owned by Madame Bachy; Reserve Dog, Voila Mister Speaker D'Alverne, bred by Mrs. Rundle and owned by Madame Desschans; Third, Hengist of Houndsmark, bred by Mrs. M. Field and owned by Lieutenant and Mrs. William B. Wood of West Germany; and Fourth, Fula Kenge of the Congo, bred by Miss Veronica Tudor-Williams and owned by Mr. E. C. M. De Reus of Holland. Winners in bitches were: World Champion, Kachina Pinta, bred by William B. Wood and owned by George C. Martin, West Germany;

International Ch. Simba's Gusty Gail d'Alverne, bred by Mrs. Mavis-Barbara Rundle, France.

Reserve Bitch, Sherry of Pine Crest, bred by Dean I. Guess, United States, and owned by Roxie and John MacNeil, West Germany; Third, Loinslair Fula Black Cap of the Congo, bred by Mrs. Brown and owned by Lieutenant and Mrs. Wood; Fourth, Fula Furor of the Congo, bred by Veronica Tudor-Williams and owned by E. C. M. de Reus; Best of Breed, Vizir D'Iwor D'antef; and Reserve, Kachina Pinata.

There is a colorful tale behind the French debut of now Ch. Tauny Simba. Mrs. Rundle had long cherished a desire to import a Basenji to France but had been unable to find just what she wanted. As it developed, she purchased a very promising male from Mrs. Drake in England. Mrs. Rundle relates humorously that Simba arrived in Nice in a crate especially hand-made, the cost of which, together with the transport fees, exceeded the price of Simba!

Simba was shown by Mrs. Rundle in Belgium, Spain, Czechoslovakia, and Italy and played a very major role in attracting admiration for the breed, which was relatively unknown in Europe in the late sixties. His self-assurance and superb poise never failed to elicit notice and praise. Prior to this time, few had ever seen a Basenji other than some of the older judges who had known them as Congo Terriers twenty-five years earlier.

Basenjis in Germany

An American couple, Mr. and Mrs. William B. Wood, are credited with owning the first Basenji champion in Germany as well as the first ever to compete in the German National Championship Show—Bundessieger 1973—and to win the Bundessieger title. This is International and German Ch. St. Erme Dancing Pony. Pony, along with a tri-color male, Hengist of Houndsmark, were the first Basenjis to be shown in Hungary. Both won their CACIBs in the 1974 Budapest show. (This, incidentally, was the seventy-fifth anniversary for the show.)

Mr. Wood, recently separated from the United States Army while still stationed in Germany, has accepted an Army civilian job near Hanau, Germany. It was the Woods' interest in promoting the breed in Europe which greatly influenced their decision to remain there. Late in 1975, the Woods imported Ch. Kukuk's Harvey Wallbanger from the United States with the intent of introducing American bloodlines into the European breedings.

It speaks well for the Woods' dedication to Basenjis that with only two Basenjis registered in Germany in 1972, eight were registered the following year, eighteen in 1974, and more than thirty in 1975. In 1973, only six Basenjis were shown in Central Europe, but more than twenty were shown in 1974-75. Since shows are far less frequent in Europe than in the United States, for instance, championship is a major accomplishment. However, with increasing interest in Germany, Spain, Italy, and Sweden, Basenjis appear destined to outgrow their reputation of being a "rare breed" in Europe.

International Champion and VDH Sieger St. Erme Dancing Pony, owned by Mr. and Mrs. William B. Wood.

95

Drawings of natives with Basenjis, by
Artist-Breeder Roberta Fredrick,
Bushveld Basenjis.

Manners for
the Family Dog

Although each dog has personality quirks and idiosyncrasies that set him apart as an individual, dogs in general have two characteristics that can be utilized to advantage in training. The first is the dog's strong desire to please, which has been built up through centuries of association with man. The second lies in the innate quality of the dog's mentality. It has been proved conclusively that while dogs have reasoning power, their learning ability is based on a direct association of cause and effect, so that they willingly repeat acts that bring pleasant results and discontinue acts that bring unpleasant results. Hence, to take fullest advantage of a dog's abilities, the trainer must make sure the dog understands a command, and then reward him when he obeys and correct him when he does wrong.

Commands should be as short as possible and should be repeated in the same way, day after day. Saying "Heel," one day, and "Come here and heel," the next will confuse the dog. *Heel, sit, stand, stay, down,* and *come* are standard terminology, and are preferable for a dog that may later be given advanced training.

Tone of voice is important, too. For instance, a coaxing tone helps cajole a young puppy into trying something new. Once an exercise is mastered, commands given in a firm, matter-of-fact voice give the dog confidence in his own ability. Praise, expressed in an exuberant tone will tell the dog quite clearly that he has earned his master's approval. On the other hand, a firm "No" indicates with equal clarity that he has done wrong.

Rewards for good performance may consist simply of praising lavishly and petting the dog, although many professional trainers use bits of food as rewards. Tidbits are effective only if the dog is hungry, of course. And if you smoke, you must be sure to wash your hands before each training session, for the odor of nicotine is repulsive to dogs. On the hands of a heavy smoker, the odor of nicotine may be so strong that the dog is unable to smell the tidbit.

Correction for wrong-doing should be limited to repeating "No," in a scolding tone of voice or to confining the dog to his bed. Spanking or striking the dog is taboo—particularly using sticks, which might cause injury, but the hand should never be used either. For field training as well as some obedience work, the hand is used to signal the dog. Dogs that have been punished by slapping have a tendency to cringe whenever they see a hand raised and consequently do not respond promptly when the owner's intent is not to punish but to signal.

Some trainers recommend correcting the dog by whacking him with a rolled-up newspaper. The idea is that the newspaper will not injure the dog but that the resulting noise will condition the dog to avoid repeating the act that seemingly caused the noise. Many authorities object to this type of correction, for it may result in the dog's becoming "noise-shy"—a decided disadvantage with show dogs which must maintain poise in adverse, often noisy, situations. "Noise-shyness" is also an unfortunate reaction in field dogs, since it may lead to gun-shyness.

To be effective, correction must be administered immediately, so that in the dog's mind there is a direct connection between his act and the correction. You can make voice corrections under almost any circumstances, but you must never call the dog to you and then correct him, or he will associate the correction with the fact that he has come and will become reluctant to respond. If the dog is at a distance and doing something he shouldn't, go to him and scold him while he is still involved in wrong-doing. If this is impossible, ignore the offense until he repeats it and you can correct him properly.

Especially while a dog is young, he should be watched closely and stopped before he gets into mischief. All dogs need to do a certain amount of chewing, so to prevent your puppy's chewing something you value, provide him with his own rubber balls and toys. Never allow him to chew cast-off slippers and then expect him to differentiate between cast-off items and those you value. Nylon stockings, wooden articles, and various other items may cause intestinal obstructions if the dog chews and swallows them, and death may result. So it is essential that the dog be permitted to chew only on bones or rubber toys.

Serious training for obedience should not be started until a dog is a year old. But basic training in house manners should begin the day the puppy enters his new home. A puppy should never be given the run of the house but should be confined to a box or small pen except for play periods when you can devote full attention to him. The first thing to teach the dog is his name, so that whenever he hears it, he will immediately come to attention. Whenever you are near his box, talk to him, using his name repeatedly. During play periods, talk to him, pet him, and handle him, for he must be conditioned so he will not object to being handled by a veterinarian, show judge, or family friend. As the dog investigates his surroundings, watch him carefully and if he tries something he shouldn't, reprimand him with a scolding "No!" If he repeats the offense, scold him and confine him to his box, then praise him. Discipline must be prompt, consistent, and always followed with praise. Never tease the dog, and never allow others to do so. Kindness and understanding are essential to a pleasant, mutually rewarding relationship.

When the puppy is two to three months old, secure a flat, narrow leather collar and have him start wearing it (never use a harness, which will encourage tugging and pulling). After a week or so, attach a light leather lead to the collar during play sessions and let the puppy walk around, dragging the lead behind him. Then start holding the end of the lead and coaxing the puppy to come to you. He will then be fully accustomed to collar and lead when you start taking him outside while he is being housebroken.

Housebreaking can be accomplished in a matter of approximately two weeks provided you wait until the dog is mature enough to have some control over bodily functions. This is usually at about four months. Until that time, the puppy should spend most of his day confined to his penned area, with the floor covered with several thicknesses of newspapers so that he may relieve himself when necessary without damage to floors.

Either of two methods works well in housebreaking—the choice depending upon where you live. If you live in a house with a readily accessible yard, you will probably want to train the puppy from the beginning to go outdoors. If you live in an apartment without easy access to a yard, you may decide to train him first to relieve himself on newspapers and then when he has learned control, to teach the puppy to go outdoors.

If you decide to train the puppy by taking him outdoors, arrange some means of confining him indoors where you can watch him closely—in a small penned area, or tied to a short lead (five or six feet). Dogs are naturally clean animals, reluctant to soil their quarters, and confining the puppy to a limited area will encourage him to avoid making a mess.

A young puppy must be taken out often, so watch your puppy closely and if he indicates he is about to relieve himself, take him out at once. If he has an accident, scold him and take him out so he will associate the act of going outside with the need to relieve himself. Always take the puppy out within an hour after meals—preferably to the same place each time—and make sure he relieves himself before you return him to the house. Restrict his water for two hours before bedtime and take him out just before you retire for the night. Then, as soon as you wake in the morning, take him out again.

For paper training, set aside a particular room and cover a large area of the floor with several thicknesses of newspapers. Confine the dog on a short leash and each time he relieves himself, remove the soiled papers and replace them with clean ones.

As his control increases, gradually decrease the paper area, leaving part of the floor bare. If he uses the bare floor, scold him mildly and put him on the papers, letting him know that there is where he is to relieve himself. As he comes to understand the idea, increase the bare area until papers cover only space equal to approximately two full newspaper sheets. Keep him using the papers, but begin taking him on a leash to the street at the times of day that he habitually relieves himself. Watch him closely when he is indoors and at the first sign that he needs to go, take him outdoors. Restrict his water for two hours before bedtime, but if necessary, permit him to use the papers before you retire for the night.

Using either method, the puppy will be housebroken in an amazingly short time. Once he has learned control he will need to relieve himself only four or five times a day.

Informal obedience training, started at the age of about six to eight months, will provide a good background for any advanced training you may decide to give your dog later. The collar most

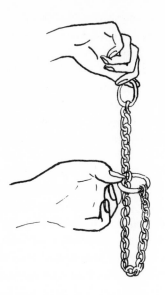

effective for training is the metal chain-link variety. The correct size for your dog will be about one inch longer than the measurement around the largest part of his head. The chain must be slipped through one of the rings so the collar forms a loop. The collar should be put on with the loose ring at the right of the dog's neck, the chain attached to it coming over the neck and through the holding ring, rather than under the neck. Since the dog is to be at your left during most of the training, this makes the collar most effective.

The leash should be attached to the loose ring, and should be either webbing or leather, six feet long and a half inch to a full inch wide. When you want your dog's attention, or wish to correct him, give a light, quick pull on the leash, which will momentarily tighten the collar about the neck. Release the pressure instantly, and the correction will have been made. If the puppy is already accustomed to a leather collar, he will adjust easily to the training collar. But before you start training sessions, practice walking with the dog until he responds readily when you increase tension on the leash.

Set aside a period of fifteen minutes, once or twice a day, for regular training sessions, and train in a place where there will be no distractions. Teach only one exercise at a time, making sure the dog has mastered it before going on to another. It will probably take at least a week for the dog to master each exercise. As training progresses, start each session by reviewing exercises the dog has already learned, then go on to the new exercise for a period of concerted practice. When discipline is required, make the correction immediately, and always praise the dog after corrections as well as when he obeys promptly. During each session stick strictly to business. Afterwards, take time to play with the dog.

The first exercise to teach is heeling. Have the dog at your left and hold the leash as shown in the illustration on the preceding page. Start walking, and just as you put your foot forward for the first step, say your dog's name to get his attention, followed by the command, "Heel!" Simultaneously, pull on the leash lightly. As you walk, try to keep the dog at your left side, with his head alongside your left leg. Pull on the leash as necessary to urge him forward or back, to right or left, but keep him in position. Each time you pull on the leash, say "Heel!" and praise the dog lavishly. When the dog heels properly in a straight line, start making circles, turning corners, etc.

Once the dog has learned to heel well, start teaching the "sit." Each time you stop while heeling, command "Sit!" The dog will be at your left, so use your left hand to press on his rear and guide him to a sitting position, while you use the leash in your right hand to keep his head up. Hold him in position for a few moments while you praise him, then give the command to heel. Walk a few steps, stop, and repeat the procedure. Before long he will automatically sit whenever you stop. You can then teach the dog to "sit" from any position.

When the dog will sit on command without correction, he is ready to learn to stay until you release him. Simply sit him, command "Stay!" and hold him in position for perhaps half a minute, repeating "Stay," if he attempts to stand. You can release him by saying "O.K." Gradually increase the time until he will stay on command for three or four minutes.

The "stand-stay" should also be taught when the dog is on leash. While you are heeling, stop and give the command "Stand!" Keep the dog from sitting by quickly placing your left arm under him, immediately in front of his right hind leg. If he continues to try to sit, don't scold him but start up again with the heel command, walk a few steps, and stop again, repeating the stand command and preventing the dog from sitting. Once the dog has mastered the stand, teach him to stay by holding him in position and repeating the word "Stay!"

The "down stay" will prove beneficial in many situations, but especially if you wish to take your dog in the car without confining him to a crate. To teach the "down," have the dog sitting at your side with collar and leash on. If he is a large dog, step forward with the leash in your hand and turn so you face him. Let the leash touch the floor, then step over it with your right foot so it is under the instep of your shoe. Grasping the leash low down with both hands, slowly pull up, saying, "Down!" Hold the leash taut until the dog goes down. Once he responds well, teach the dog to stay in the down position (the down-stay), using the same method as for the sit- and stand-stays.

To teach small dogs the "down," another method may be used. Have the dog sit at your side, then kneel beside him. Reach across his back with your left arm, and take hold of his left front leg close to the body. At the same time, with your right hand take hold of his right front leg close to his body. As you command "Down!" gently lift the legs and place the dog in the down position. Release your hold on his legs and slide your left hand onto his back, repeating, "Down, stay," while keeping him in position.

The "come" is taught when the dog is on leash and heeling. Simply walk along, then suddenly take a step backward, saying "Come!" Pull the leash as you give the command and the dog will turn and follow you. Continue walking backward, repeatedly saying "Come," and tightening the leash if necessary.

Once the dog has mastered the exercises while on leash, try taking the leash off and going through the same routine, beginning with the heeling exercise. If the dog doesn't respond promptly, he needs review with the leash on. But patience and persistence will be rewarded, for you will have a dog you can trust to respond promptly under all conditions.

Even after they are well trained, dogs sometimes develop bad habits that are hard to break. Jumping on people is a common habit, and all members of the family must assist if it is to be broken. If the dog is a large or medium breed, take a step forward and raise your knee just as he starts to jump on you. As your knee strikes the dog's chest, command "Down!" in a scolding voice. When a small dog jumps on you, take both front paws in your hands, and, while talking in a pleasant tone of voice, step on the dog's back feet just hard enough to hurt them slightly. With either method the dog is taken by surprise and doesn't associate the discomfort with the person causing it.

Occasionally a dog may be too chummy with guests who don't care for dogs. If the dog has had obedience training, simply command "Come!" When he responds, have him sit beside you.

Excessive barking is likely to bring complaints from neighbors, and persistent efforts may be needed to subdue a dog that barks without provocation. To correct the habit, you must be close to the dog when he starts barking. Encircle his muzzle with both hands, hold his mouth shut, and command "Quiet!" in a firm voice. He should soon learn to respond so you can control him simply by giving the command.

Sniffing other dogs is an annoying habit. If the dog is off leash and sniffs other dogs, ignoring your commands to come, he needs to review the lessons on basic behavior. When the dog is on leash, scold him, then pull on the leash, command "Heel," and walk away from the other dog.

A well-trained dog will be no problem if you decide to take him with you when you travel. No matter how well he responds, however, he should never be permitted off leash when you walk him in a strange area. Distractions will be more tempting, and there will be more chance of his being attacked by other dogs. So whenever the dog travels with you, take his collar and leash along—and use them.

Bench Shows

Centuries ago, it was common practice to hold agricultural fairs in conjunction with spring and fall religious festivals, and to these gatherings, cattle, dogs, and other livestock were brought for exchange. As time went on, it became customary to provide entertainment, too. Dogs often participated in such sporting events as bull baiting, bear baiting, and ratting. Then the dog that exhibited the greatest skill in the arena was also the one that brought the highest price when time came for barter or sale. Today, these fairs seem a far cry from our highly organized bench shows and field trials. But they were the forerunners of modern dog shows and played an important role in shaping the development of purebred dogs.

The first organized dog show was held at Newcastle, England, in 1859. Later that same year, a show was held at Birmingham. At both shows dogs were divided into four classes and only Pointers and Setters were entered. In 1860, the first dog show in Germany was held at Apoldo, where nearly one hundred dogs were exhibited and entries were divided into six groups. Interest expanded rapidly, and by the time the Paris Exhibition was held in 1878, the dog show was a fixture of international importance.

In the United States, the first organized bench show was held in 1874 in conjunction with the meeting of the Illinois State Sportsmen's Association in Chicago, and all entries were dogs of sporting breeds. Although the show was a rather casual affair, interest spread quickly. Before the end of the year, shows were held in Oswego, New York, Mineola, Long Island, and Memphis, Tennessee. And the latter combined a bench show with the first organized field trial ever held in the United States. In January 1875, an all-breed show (the first in the United States) was held at Detroit, Michigan. From then on, interest increased rapidly, though rules were not always uniform, for there was no organization through which to coordinate activities until September 1884

Benching area at Westminster Kennel Club Show.

Judging for Best in Show at Westminster Kennel Club Show.

when The American Kennel Club was founded. Now the largest dog registering organization in the world, the A.K.C. is an association of several hundred member clubs—all breed, specialty, field trial, and obedience groups—each represented by a delegate to the A.K.C.

The several thousand shows and trials held annually in the United States do much to stimulate interest in breeding to produce better looking, sounder, purebred dogs. For breeders, shows provide a means of measuring the merits of their work as compared with accomplishments of other breeders. For hundreds of thousands of dog fanciers, they provide an absorbing hobby.

For both spectators and participating owners, field trials constitute a fascinating demonstration of dogs competing under actual hunting conditions, where emphasis is on excellence of performance. The trials are sponsored by clubs or associations of persons interested in hunting dogs. Trials for Pointing breeds, Dachshunds, Retrievers, Spaniels, and Beagles are under the jurisdiction of The American Kennel Club and information concerning such activities is published in "Pure Bred Dogs—American Kennel Gazette." Trials for Bird Dogs are run by rules and regulations of the Amateur Field Trial Clubs of America and information concerning them is published in "The American Field."

All purebred dogs of recognized breeds may be registered with The American Kennel Club and those of hunting breeds may also be registered with The American Field. Dogs that have won championships both in the field and in bench shows are known as dual champions.

At bench (or conformation) shows, dogs are rated comparatively on their physical qualities (or conformation) in accordance with breed Standards which have been approved by The American Kennel Club. Characteristics such as size, coat, color, placement of eye or ear, general soundness, etc., are the basis for selecting the best dog in a class. Only purebred dogs are eligible to compete and if the show is one where points toward a championship are to be awarded, a dog must be at least six months old.

Bench shows are of various types. An all-breed show has classes for all of the breeds recognized by The American Kennel Club as well as a Miscellaneous Class for breeds not recognized, such as the Australian Cattle Dog, the Ibizan Hound, the Spinoni Italiani, the Tibetan Terrier, etc. A sanctioned match is an informal meeting where dogs compete but not for championship points. A specialty show is confined to a single breed. Other shows may restrict entries to champions of record, to American-bred dogs, etc. Competition for Junior Showmanship or for Best Brace, Best Team, or Best Local Dog may be included. Also, obedience competition is held in conjunction with many bench shows.

The term "bench show" is somewhat confusing in that shows of this type may be either "benched" or "unbenched." At the former, each dog is assigned an individual numbered stall where he must remain throughout the show except for times when he is being judged, groomed, or exercised. At unbenched shows, no stalls are provided and dogs are kept in their owners' cars or in crates when not being judged.

A show where a dog is judged for conformation actually constitutes an elimination contest. To begin with, the dogs of a single breed compete with others of their breed in one of the regular classes: Puppy, Novice, Bred by Exhibitor, American-Bred, or Open, and, finally, Winners, where the top dogs of the preceding five classes meet. The next step is the judging for Best of Breed (or Best of Variety of Breed). Here the Winners Dog and Winners Bitch (or the dog named Winners if only one prize is awarded) compete with any champions that are entered, together with any undefeated dogs that have competed in additional non-regular classes. The dog named Best of Breed (or Best of Variety of Breed), then goes on to compete with the other Best of Breed winners in his Group. The dogs that win in Group competition then compete for the final and highest honor, Best in Show.

When the Winners Class is divided by sex, championship points are awarded the Winners Dog and Winners Bitch. If the Winners Class is not divided by sex, championship points are awarded the dog or bitch named Winners. The number of points awarded varies, depending upon such factors as the number of dogs competing, the Schedule of Points established by the Board of Directors of the A.K.C., and whether the dog goes on to win Best of Breed, the Group, and Best in Show.

In order to become a champion, a dog must win fifteen points, including points from at least two major wins—that is, at least two shows where three or more points are awarded. The major wins must be under two different judges, and one or more of the remaining points must be won under a third judge. The most points ever awarded at a show is five and the least is one, so, in order to become

Junior Showmanship Competition at Westminster Kennel Club Show.

a champion, a dog must be exhibited and win in at least three shows, and usually he is shown many times before he wins his championship.

"Pure Bred Dogs—American Kennel Gazette" and other dog magazines contain lists of forthcoming shows, together with names and addresses of sponsoring organizations to which you may write for entry forms and information relative to fees, closing dates, etc. Before entering your dog in a show for the first time, you should familiarize yourself with the regulations and rules governing competition. You may secure such information from The American Kennel Club or from a local dog club specializing in your breed. It is essential that you also familiarize yourself with the A.K.C. approved Standard for your breed so you will be fully aware of characteristics worthy of merit as well as those considered faulty, or possibly even serious enough to disqualify the dog from competition. For instance, monorchidism (failure of one testicle to descend) and cryptorchidism (failure of both testicles to descend) are disqualifying faults in all breeds.

If possible, you should first attend a show as a spectator and observe judging procedures from ringside. It will also be helpful to join a local breed club and to participate in sanctioned matches before entering an all-breed show.

The dog should be equipped with a narrow leather show lead and a show collar—never an ornamented or spiked collar. For benched shows, a metal-link bench chain will be needed to fasten the dog to the bench. For unbenched shows, the dog's crate should be taken along so that he may be confined in comfort when he is not appearing in the ring. A dog should never be left in a car with all the windows closed. In hot weather the temperature will become unbearable in a very short time. Heat exhaustion may result from even a short period of confinement, and death may ensue.

Food and water dishes will be needed, as well as a supply of the food and water to which the dog is accustomed. Brushes and combs are also necessary, so that you may give the dog's coat a final grooming after you arrive at the show.

Familiarize yourself with the schedule of classes ahead of time, for the dog must be fed and exercised and permitted to relieve himself, and any last-minute grooming completed before his class is called. Both you and the dog should be ready to enter the ring unhurriedly. A good deal of skill in conditioning, training, and handling is required if a dog is to be presented properly. And it is essential that the handler himself be composed, for a jittery handler will transmit his nervousness to his dog.

Once the class is assembled in the ring, the judge will ask that the dogs be paraded in line, moving counter-clockwise in a circle. If you have trained your dog well, you will have no difficulty controlling him in the ring, where he must change pace quickly and gracefully and walk and trot elegantly and proudly with head erect. The show dog must also stand quietly for inspection, posing like a statue for several minutes while the judge observes his structure in detail, examines teeth, feet, coat, etc. When the judge calls your dog forward for individual inspection, do not attempt to converse, but answer any questions he may ask.

As the judge examines the class, he measures each dog against the ideal described in the Standard, then measures the dogs against each other in a comparative sense and selects for first place the dog that comes closest to conforming to the Standard for its breed. If your dog isn't among the winners, don't grumble. If he places first, don't brag loudly. For a bad loser is disgusting, but a poor winner is insufferable.

Obedience Competition

For hundreds of years, dogs have been used in England and Germany in connection with police and guard work, and their working potential has been evaluated through tests devised to show agility, strength, and courage. Organized training has also been popular with English and German breeders for many years, although it was first practiced primarily for the purpose of training large breeds in aggressive tactics.

There was little interest in obedience training in the United States until 1933 when Mrs. Whitehouse Walker returned from England and enthusiastically introduced the sport. Two years later, Mrs. Walker persuaded The American Kennel Club to approve organized obedience activities and to assume jurisdiction over obedience rules. Since then, interest has increased at a phenomenal rate, for obedience competition is not only a sport the average spectator can follow readily, but also a sport for which the average owner can train his own dog easily. Obedience competition is suitable for all breeds. Furthermore, there is no limit to the number of dogs that may win in competition, for each dog is scored individually on the basis of a point rating system.

The dog is judged on his response to certain commands, and if he gains a high enough score in three successive trials under different judges, he wins an obedience degree. Degrees awarded are "C.D."—Companion Dog; "C.D.X."—Companion Dog Excellent; and "U.D." —Utility Dog. A fourth degree, the "T.D.," or Tracking Dog degree, may be won at any time and tests for it are held apart from dog shows. The qualifying score is a minimum of 170 points out of a possible total of 200, with no score in any one exercise less than 50% of the points allotted.

Since obedience titles are progressive, earlier titles (with the exception of the tracking degree) are dropped as a dog acquires the next higher degree. If an obedience title is gained in another country in addition to the United States, that fact is signified by the word "International," followed by the title.

Trials for obedience trained dogs are held at most of the larger bench shows, and obedience training clubs are to be found in almost all communities today. Information concerning forthcoming trials and lists of obedience training clubs are included regularly in "Pure Bred Dogs—American Kennel Gazette"—and other dog magazines. Pamphlets containing rules and regulations governing obedience competition are available upon request from The American Kennel Club, 51 Madison Avenue, New York, N.Y. 10010. Rules are revised occasionally, so if you are interested in participating in obedience competition, you should be sure your copy of the regulations is current.

All dogs must comply with the same rules, although in broad jump, high jump, and bar jump competition, the jumps are adjusted to the size of the breed. Classes at obedience trials are divided into Novice (A and B), Open (A and B), and Utility (which may be divided into A and B, at the option of the sponsoring club and with the approval of The American Kennel Club).

The Novice class is for dogs that have not won the title Companion Dog. In Novice A, no person who has previously handled a dog that has won a C.D. title in the obedience ring at a licensed or member trial, and no person who has regularly trained such a dog, may enter or handle a dog. The handler must be the dog's owner or a member of the owner's immediate family. In Novice B, dogs may be handled by the owner or any other person.

The Open A class is for dogs that have won the C.D. title but have not won the C.D.X. title. Obedience judges and licensed handlers may not enter or handle dogs in this class. Each dog must be handled by the owner or by a member of his immediate family. The Open B class is for dogs that have won the title C.D. or C.D.X. A dog may continue to compete in this class after it has won the title U.D. Dogs in this class may be handled by the owner or any other person.

The Utility class is for dogs that have won the title C.D.X. Dogs that have won the title U.D. may continue to compete in this class, and dogs may be handled by the owner or any other person. Provided the A.K.C. approves, a club may choose to divide the Utility class into Utility A and Utility B. When this is done, the Utility A class is for dogs that have won the title C.D.X. and have not won the title U.D. Obedience judges and licensed handlers may not enter or handle dogs in this class. All other dogs that are eligible for the Utility class but not eligible for Utility A may be entered in Utility B.

Novice competition includes such exercises as heeling on and off lead, the stand for examination, coming on recall, and the long sit and the long down.

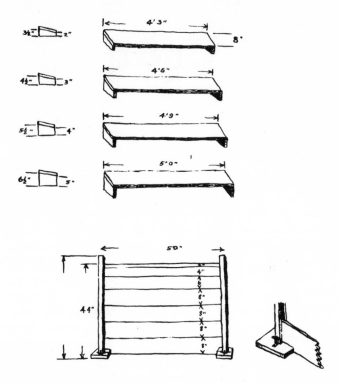

Broad jump and solid hurdle.

In Open competition, the dog must perform such exercises as heeling free, the drop on recall, and the retrieve on the flat and over the high jump. Also, he must execute the broad jump, and the long sit and long down.

In the Utility class, competition includes scent discrimination, the directed retrieve, the signal exercise, directed jumping, and the group examination.

Tracking is the most difficult test. It is always done out-of-doors, of course, and, for obvious reasons, cannot be held at a dog show. The dog must follow a scent trail that is about a quarter mile in length. He is also required to find a scent object (glove, wallet, or other article) left by a stranger who has walked the course to lay down the scent. The dog is required to follow the trail a half to two hours after the scent is laid.

An ideal way to train a dog for obedience competition is to join an obedience class or a training club. In organized class work, beginners' classes cover pretty much the same exercises as those

113

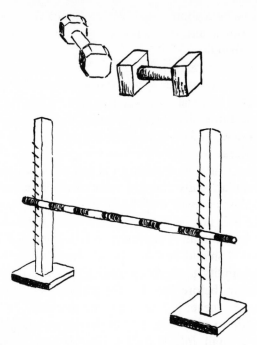

Dumbbells and bar jump.

described in the chapter on training. However, through class work you will develop greater precision than is possible in training your dog by yourself. Amateur handlers often cause the dog to be penalized, for if the handler fails to abide by the rules, it is the dog that suffers the penalty. A common infraction of the rules is using more than one signal or command where regulations stipulate only one may be used. Classwork will help eliminate such errors, which the owner may make unconsciously if he is working alone. Working with a class will also acquaint both dog and handler with ring procedure so that obedience trials will not present unforeseen problems.

Thirty or forty owners and dogs often comprise a class, and exercises are performed in unison, with individual instruction provided if it is required. The procedure followed in training—in fact, even wording of various commands—may vary from instructor to instructor. Equipment used will vary somewhat, also, but will usually include a training collar and leash such as those shown on page 109, a long line, a dumbbell, and a jumping stick.

The latter may be a short length of heavy doweling or a broom handle and both it and the dumbbell are usually painted white for increased visibility.

A bitch in season must never be taken to a training class, so before enrolling a female dog, you should determine whether she may be expected to come into season before classes are scheduled to end. If you think she will, it is better to wait and enroll her in a later course, rather than start the course and then miss classes for several weeks.

In addition to the time devoted to actual work in class, the dog must have regular, daily training sessions for practice at home. Before each class or home training session, the dog should be exercised so he will not be highly excited when the session starts, and he must be given an opportunity to relieve himself before the session begins. (Should he have an accident during the class, it is your responsibility to clean up after him.) The dog should be fed several hours before time for the class to begin or else after the class is over—never just before going to class.

If you decide to enter your dog in obedience competition, it is well to enter a small, informal show the first time. Dogs are usually called in the order in which their names appear in the catalog, so as soon as you arrive at the show, acquaint yourself with the schedule. If your dog is not the first to be judged, spend some time at ringside, observing the routine so you will know what to expect when your dog's turn comes.

In addition to collar, leash, and other equipment, you should take your dog's food and water pans and a supply of the food and water to which he is accustomed. You should also take his brushes and combs in order to give him a last-minute brushing before you enter the ring. It is important that the dog look his best even though he isn't to be judged on his appearance.

Before entering the ring, exercise your dog, give him a drink of water, and permit him to relieve himself. Once your dog enters the ring, give him your full attention and be sure to give voice commands distinctly so he will hear and understand, for there will be many distractions at ringside.

Top dogs in Utility Class. This illustrates variety of breeds that compete in obedience.

Genetics

Genetics, the science of heredity, deals with the processes by which physical and mental traits of parents are transmitted to offspring. For centuries, man has been trying to solve these puzzles, but only in the last two hundred years has significant progress been made.

During the eighteenth century, Kölreuter, a German scientist, made revolutionary discoveries concerning plant sexuality and hybridization but was unable to explain just how hereditary processes worked. In the middle of the nineteenth century, Gregor Johann Mendel, an Augustinian monk, experimented with the ordinary garden pea and made other discoveries of major significance. He found that an inherited characteristic was inherited as a complete unit, and that certain characteristics predominated over others. Next, he observed that the hereditary characteristics of each parent are contained in each offspring, even when they are not visible, and that "hidden" characteristics can be transferred without change in their nature to the grandchildren, or even later generations. Finally, he concluded that although heredity contains an element of uncertainty, some things are predictable on the basis of well-defined mathematical laws.

Unfortunately, Mendel's published paper went unheeded, and when he died in 1884 he was still virtually unknown to the scientific world. But other researchers were making discoveries, too. In 1900, three different scientists reported to learned societies that much of their research in hereditary principles had been proved years before by Gregor Mendel and that findings matched perfectly.

Thus, hereditary traits were proved to be transmitted through the chromosomes found in pairs in every living being, one of each pair contributed by the mother, the other by the father. Within each chromosome have been found hundreds of smaller structures, or genes, which are the actual determinants of hereditary characteristics. Some genes are dominant and will be seen in the offspring. Others are recessive and will not be outwardly apparent, yet can be passed on to the offspring to combine with a similar recessive gene of the other parent and thus be seen. Or they may be passed on to the offspring, not be outwardly apparent, but be passed on again to become apparent in a later generation.

Once the genetic theory of inheritance became widely known, scientists began drawing a well-defined line between inheritance and environment. More recent studies show some overlapping of these influences and indicate a combination of the two may be responsible for certain characteristics. For instance, studies have proved that extreme cold increases the amount of black pigment in the skin and hair of the "Himalayan" rabbit, although it has little or no effect on the white or colored rabbit. Current research also indicates that even though characteristics are determined by the genes, some environmental stress occurring at a particular period of pregnancy might cause physical change in the embryo.

Long before breeders had any knowledge of genetics, they practiced one of its most important principles—selective breeding. Experience quickly showed that "like begets like," and by breeding like with like and discarding unlike offspring, the various individual breeds were developed to the point where variations were relatively few. Selective breeding is based on the idea of maintaining the quality of a breed at the highest possible level, while improving whatever defects are prevalent. It requires that only the top dogs in a litter be kept for later breeding, and that inferior specimens be ruthlessly eliminated.

In planning any breeding program, the first requisite is a definite goal—that is, to have clearly in mind a definite picture of the type of dog you wish eventually to produce. To attempt to breed perfection is to approach the problem unrealistically. But if you don't breed for improvement, it is preferable that you not breed at all.

As a first step, you should select a bitch that exemplifies as many of the desired characteristics as possible and mate her with a dog that also has as many of the desired characteristics as possible. If you start with mediocre pets, you will produce mediocre pet puppies. If you decide to start with more than one bitch, all should closely approach the type you desire, since you will

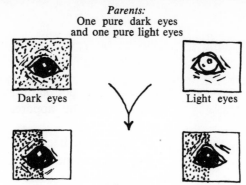

Parents:
One pure dark eyes
and one pure light eyes

Dark eyes · Light eyes

Offspring:
Eyes dark (dominant) with light recessive

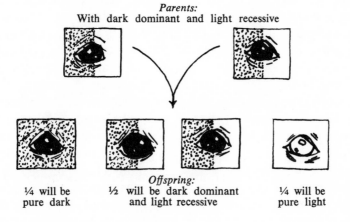

Parents:
With dark dominant and light recessive

¼ will be
pure dark

Offspring:
½ will be dark dominant
and light recessive

¼ will be
pure light

The above is a schematic representation of the Mendelian law as it applies to the inheritance of eye color. The law applies in the same way to the inheritance of other physical characteristics.

then stand a better chance of producing uniformly good puppies from all. Breeders often start with a single bitch and keep the best bitches in every succeeding generation.

Experienced breeders look for "prepotency" in breeding stock —that is, the ability of a dog or bitch to transmit traits to most or all of its offspring. While the term is usually used to describe the transmission of good qualities, a dog may also be prepotent in transmitting faults. To be prepotent in a practical sense, a dog must possess many characteristics controlled by dominant genes. If desired characteristics are recessive, they will be apparent in the offspring only if carried by both sire and dam. Prepotent dogs and bitches usually come from a line of prepotent ancestors, but the mere fact that a dog has exceptional ancestors will not necessarily mean that he himself will produce exceptional offspring.

A single dog may sire a tremendous number of puppies, whereas a bitch can produce only a comparatively few litters during her lifetime. Thus, a sire's influence may be very widespread as compared to that of a bitch. But in evaluating a particular litter, it must be remembered that the bitch has had as much influence as has had the dog.

Inbreeding, line-breeding, outcrossing, or a combination of the three are the methods commonly used in selective breeding.

Inbreeding is the mating together of closely related animals, such as father-daughter, mother-son, or brother-sister. Although some breeders insist such breeding will lead to the production of defective individuals, it is through rigid inbreeding that all breeds of dogs have been established. Controlled tests have shown that any harmful effects appear within the first five or ten generations, and that if rigid selection is exercised from the beginning, a vigorous inbred strain will be built up.

Line-breeding is also the mating together of individuals related by family lines. However, matings are made not so much on the basis of the dog's and bitch's relationship to each other, but, instead, on the basis of their relationship to a highly admired ancestor, with a view to perpetuating his qualities. Line-breeding constitutes a long-range program and cannot be accomplished in a single generation.

Outcrossing is the breeding together of two dogs that are unrelated in family lines. Actually, since breeds have been developed through the mating of close relatives, all dogs within any given breed are related to some extent. There are few breedings that are true outcrosses, but if there is no common ancestor within five generations, a mating is usually considered an outcross.

Experienced breeders sometimes outcross for one generation in order to eliminate a particular fault, then go back to inbreeding or line-breeding. Neither the good effects nor the bad effects of outcrossing can be truly evaluated in a single mating, for undesirable recessive traits may be introduced into a strain, yet not show up for several generations. Outcrossing is better left to experienced breeders, for continual outcrossing results in a wide variation in type and great uncertainty as to the results that may be expected.

Two serious defects that are believed heritable—subluxation and orchidism—should be zealously guarded against, and afflicted dogs and their offspring should be eliminated from breeding programs. Subluxation is a condition of the hip joint where the bone of the socket is eroded and the head of the thigh bone is also worn away, causing lameness which becomes progressively more serious until the dog is unable to walk. Orchidism is the failure of one or both testicles to develop and descend properly. When one testicle is involved, the term "monorchid" is used. When both are involved, "cryptorchid" is used. A cryptorchid is almost always sterile, whereas a monorchid is usually fertile. There is evidence that orchidism "runs in families" and that a monorchid transmits the tendency through bitch and male puppies alike.

Through the years, many misconceptions concerning heredity have been perpetuated. Perhaps the one most widely perpetuated is the idea evolved hundreds of years ago that somehow characteristics were passed on through the mixing of the blood of the parents. We still use terminology evolved from that theory when we speak of bloodlines, or describe individuals as full-blooded, despite the fact that the theory was disproved more than a century ago.

Also inaccurate and misleading is any statement that a definite fraction or proportion of an animal's inherited characteristics can be positively attributed to a particular ancestor. Individuals lacking knowledge of genetics sometimes declare that an individual receives half his inherited characteristics from each parent, a quarter from each grandparent, an eighth from each great-grandparent, etc. Thousands of volumes of scientific findings have been published, but no simple way has been found to determine positively which characteristics have been inherited from which ancestors, for the science of heredity is infinitely complex.

Any breeder interested in starting a serious breeding program should study several of the excellent books on canine genetics that are currently available.

Whelping box. Detail at right shows proper side-wall construction which helps keep small puppies confined and provides sheltered nook which to prevent crushing or smothering.

Breeding and Whelping

The breeding life of a bitch begins when she comes into season the first time at the age of about one to two years (depending on what breed she is). Thereafter, she will come in season at roughly six-month intervals, but this, too, is subject to variation. Her maximum fertility builds up from puberty to full maturity and then declines until a state of total sterility is reached in old age. Just when this occurs is hard to determine, for the fact that an older bitch shows signs of being in season doesn't necessarily mean she is still capable of reproducing.

The length of the season varies from eighteen to twenty-one days. The first indication is a pronounced swelling of the vulva with coincidental bleeding (called "showing color") for about the first seven to nine days. The discharge gradually turns to a creamy color, and it is during this phase (estrus), from about the tenth to the fifteenth days, that the bitch is ovulating and is receptive to the male. The ripe, unfertilized ova survive for about seventy-two hours. If fertilization doesn't occur, the ova die and are discharged the next time the bitch comes in season. If fertilization does take place, each ovum attaches itself to the walls of the uterus, a membrane forms to seal it off, and a foetus develops from it.

Following the estrus phase, the bitch is still in season until about the twenty-first day and will continue to be attractive to males, although she will usually fight them off as she did the first few days. Nevertheless, to avoid accidental mating, the bitch must be confined for the entire period. Virtual imprisonment is necessary, for male dogs display uncanny abilities in their efforts to reach a bitch in season.

The odor that attracts the males is present in the bitch's urine, so it is advisable to take her a good distance from the house before permitting her to relieve herself. To eliminate problems completely, your veterinarian can prescribe a preparation that will disguise the odor but will not interfere with breeding when the time is right. Many fanciers use such preparations when exhibiting a bitch and find that nearby males show no interest whatsoever. But it is not advisable to permit a bitch to run loose when she has been given a product of this type, for during estrus she will seek the company of male dogs and an accidental mating may occur.

A potential brood bitch, regardless of breed, should have good bone, ample breadth and depth of ribbing, and adequate room in the pelvic region. Unless a bitch is physically mature—well beyond the puppy stage when she has her first season—breeding should be delayed until her second or a later season. Furthermore, even though it is possible for a bitch to conceive twice a year, she should not be bred oftener than once a year. A bitch that is bred too often will age prematurely and her puppies are likely to lack vigor.

Two or three months before a bitch is to be mated, her physical condition should be considered carefully. If she is too thin, provide a rich, balanced diet plus the regular exercise needed to develop strong, supple muscles. Daily exercise on the lead is as necessary for the too-thin bitch as for the too fat one, although the latter will need more exercise and at a brisker pace, as well as a reduction of food, if she is to be brought to optimum condition. A prospective brood bitch must have had permanent distemper shots as well as rabies vaccination. And a month before her season is due, a veterinarian should examine a stool specimen for worms. If there is evidence of infestation, the bitch should be wormed.

A dog may be used at stud from the time he reaches physical maturity, well on into old age. The first time your bitch is bred, it is well to use a stud that has already proven his ability by having sired other litters. The fact that a neighbor's dog is readily available should not influence your choice, for to produce the best puppies, you must select the stud most suitable from a genetic standpoint.

If the stud you prefer is not going to be available at the time your bitch is to be in season, you may wish to consult your veterinarian concerning medications available for inhibiting the onset of the season. With such preparations, the bitch's season can be delayed indefinitely.

Usually the first service will be successful. However, if it isn't, in most cases an additional service is given free, provided the stud dog is still in the possession of the same owner. If the bitch misses, it may be because her cycle varies widely from normal. Through microscopic examination, a veterinarian can determine exactly when the bitch is entering the estrus phase and thus is likely to conceive.

The owner of the stud should give you a stud-service certificate, providing a four-generation pedigree for the sire and showing the date of mating. The litter registration application is completed only after the puppies are whelped, but it, too, must be signed by the owner of the stud as well as the owner of the bitch. Registration forms may be secured by writing The American Kennel Club.

In normal pregnancy there is usually visible enlargement of the abdomen by the end of the fifth week. By palpation (feeling with the fingers) a veterinarian may be able to distinguish developing puppies as early as three weeks after mating, but it is unwise for a novice to poke and prod, and try to detect the presence of unborn puppies.

The gestation period normally lasts nine weeks, although it may vary from sixty-one to sixty-five days. If it goes beyond sixty-five days from the date of mating, a veterinarian should be consulted.

During the first four or five weeks, the bitch should be permitted her normal amount of activity. As she becomes heavier, she should be walked on the lead, but strenuous running and jumping should be avoided. Her diet should be well balanced (see page 43), and if she should become constipated, small amounts of mineral oil may be added to her food.

A whelping box should be secured about two weeks before the puppies are due, and the bitch should start then to use it as her bed so she will be accustomed to it by the time puppies arrive. Preferably, the box should be square, with each side long enough so that the bitch can stretch out full length and have several inches to spare at either end. The bottom should be padded with an old cotton rug or other material that is easily laundered. Edges of the padding should be tacked to the floor of the box so the puppies will not get caught in it and smother. Once it is obvious labor is about to begin, the padding should be covered with several layers of spread-out newspapers. Then, as papers become soiled, the top layer can be pulled off, leaving the area clean.

Forty-eight to seventy-two hours before the litter is to be whelped, a definite change in the shape of the abdomen will be noted. Instead of looking barrel-shaped, the abdomen will sag pendulously. Breasts usually redden and become enlarged, and milk may be present a day or two before the puppies are whelped. As the time becomes imminent, the bitch will probably scratch and root at her bedding in an effort to make a nest, and will refuse food and ask to be let out every few minutes. But the surest sign is a drop in temperature of two or three degrees about twelve hours before labor begins.

The bitch's abdomen and flanks will contract sharply when labor actually starts, and for a few minutes she will attempt to expel a puppy, then rest for a while and try again. Someone should stay with the bitch the entire time whelping is taking place, and if she appears to be having unusual difficulties, a veterinarian should be called.

Puppies are usually born head first, though some may be born feet first and no difficulty encountered. Each puppy is enclosed in a separate membranous sac that the bitch will remove with her teeth. She will sever the umbilical cord, which will be attached to the soft, spongy afterbirth that is expelled right after the puppy emerges. Usually the bitch eats the afterbirth, so it is necessary to watch and make sure one is expelled for each puppy whelped. If afterbirth is retained, the bitch may develop peritonitis and die.

The dam will lick and nuzzle each newborn puppy until it is warm and dry and ready to nurse. If puppies arrive so close together that she can't take care of them, you can help her by rubbing the puppies dry with a soft cloth. If several have been whelped but the bitch continues to be in labor, all but one should be removed and placed in a small box lined with clean towels and warmed to about seventy degrees. The bitch will be calmer if one puppy is left with her at all times.

Whelping sometimes continues as long as twenty-four hours for a very large litter, but a litter of two or three puppies may be whelped in an hour. When the bitch settles down, curls around the puppies and nuzzles them to her, it usually indicates that all have been whelped.

The bitch should be taken away for a few minutes while you clean the box and arrange clean padding. If her coat is soiled, sponge it clean before she returns to the puppies. Once she is back in the box, offer her a bowl of warm beef broth and a pan of cool water, placing both where she will not have to get up in order to reach them. As soon as she indicates interest in food, give her a generous bowl of chopped meat to which codliver oil and dicalcium phosphate have been added (see page 43).

If inadequate amounts of calcium are provided during the period the puppies are nursing, eclampsia may develop. Symptoms are violent trembling, rapid rise in temperature, and rigidity of muscles. Veterinary assistance must be secured immediately, for death may result in a very short time. Treatment consists of massive doses of calcium gluconate administered intravenously, after which symptoms subside in a miraculously short time.

All puppies are born blind and their eyes open when they are ten to fourteen days old. At first the eyes have a bluish cast and appear weak, and the puppies must be protected from strong light until at least ten days after the eyes open.

To ensure proper emotional development, young dogs should be shielded from loud noises and rough handling. Being lifted by the front legs is painful and may result in permanent injury to the shoulders. So when lifting a puppy, always place one hand under the chest with the forefinger between the front legs, and place the other hand under his bottom.

Sometimes the puppies' nails are so long and sharp that they scratch the bitch's breasts. Since the nails are soft, they can be trimmed with ordinary scissors.

If of a breed that ordinarily has a docked tail, puppies should have their tails shortened when they are three days old. Dewclaws—thumblike appendages appearing on the inside of the legs of some breeds—are removed at the same time. While both are simple procedures, they shouldn't be attempted by amateurs.

In certain breeds it is customary to crop the ears, also. This should be done at about eight weeks of age. Cropping should never be attempted by anyone other than a veterinarian, for it requires use of anesthesia and knowledge of surgical techniques, as well as judgment as to the eventual size of the dog and proportion of ear to be removed so the head will be balanced when the dog is mature.

At about four weeks of age, formula should be provided. The amount fed each day should be increased over a period of two weeks, when the puppies can be weaned completely. The formula should be prepared as described on page 41, warmed to lukewarm, and poured into a shallow pan placed on the floor of the box. After his mouth has been dipped into the mixture a few times, a puppy will usually start to lap formula. All puppies should be allowed to eat from the same pan, but be sure the small ones get their share. If they are pushed aside, feed them separately. Permit the puppies to nurse part of the time, but gradually increase the number of meals of formula. By the time the puppies are five weeks old, the dam should be allowed with them only at night. When they are about six weeks old, they should be weaned completely and fed the puppy diet described on page 41.

Once they are weaned, puppies should be given temporary distemper injections every two weeks until they are old enough for permanent inoculations. At six weeks, stool specimens should be checked for worms, for almost without exception, puppies become infested. Specimens should be checked again at eight weeks, and as often thereafter as your veterinarian recommends.

Sometimes owners decide as a matter of convenience to have a bitch spayed or a male castrated. While this is recommended when a dog has a serious inheritable defect or when abnormalities of reproductive organs develop, in sound, normal purebred dogs, spaying a bitch or castrating a male may prove a definite disadvantage. The operations automatically bar dogs from competing in shows as well as precluding use for breeding. The operations are seldom dangerous, but they should not be performed without good reason.